The Guid Scots Tongue

David Murison

DAVID MURISON was born in Fraserburgh in Buchan where a strongly marked dialect of Scots is still widely spoken. He is a graduate in Classical Philology of the Universities of Aberdeen and Cambridge. He was a Lecturer in Greek at the University of Aberdeen, Lecturer in Scottish Language at the Universities of Aberdeen and St Andrews, and from 1975 until his retirement in 1978 he was Reader in English Language at the University of Glasgow.

The author succeeded Dr William Grant as Editor of *The Scottish National Dictionary* in 1946 and completed the work in 1976. He has contributed material on Scottish language and literature to various books and periodicals and to B.B.C. broadcasts.

D1347708

Cover illustration from The Scottish National Dictionary

THE
GUID SCOTS
TONGUE

David Murison

WILLIAM BLACKWOOD

First published in 1977 by
William Blackwood & Sons Ltd
32 Thistle Street
Edinburgh EH2 1HA
Scotland

Reprinted with revisions 1978

ISBN 0 85158 121 8

Printed at the Press of
the Publisher

Contents

A map showing the area in which Lowland Scots is spoken appears on pages 34-35, for which acknowledgement is due to The Scottish National Dictionary.

Where and When Did It Start?

The most convenient date at which to begin our history of Scots is about A.D. 450 when tribes from north-west Germany, the Angles and the Saxons, crossed the North Sea, first on raiding expeditions and later to make permanent settlements in the Thames area. Speaking different dialects of the same Germanic language, they pushed northwards and westwards, driving the previous inhabitants—who were Romanised Britons speaking what the learned call a p-Celtic language—into Devon, the Pennines and the hills of Wales. The Saxons kept mostly to the south and west, as all the areas with -*sex* in their names still attest, while the Angles spread northwards through Yorkshire and Northumberland, where they formed small kingdoms, and ultimately crossed the Tweed. In 638 they captured the fortress called in the British tongue *Din Eidyn*, which they translated into their own language as Edinburgh.

This territory remained the core of Anglo-Saxon Scotland, dotted over with farm and family settlements called *hams* and *tuns*—hence place-names like Coldingham, Tyningham, Whittingehame, Haddington, Mordington, Ednam (Edenham) and Edrom (Edderham).

To the west lay the British kingdom of Strathclyde and for four hundred years the Angles made fitful attempts to control that region with varying success, except through their church which, though originally a mission from the Celtic church of Iona, had set up on its own under Cuthbert at Lindisfarne and established a bishopric at Whithorn, an Anglo-Saxon name meaning 'White House'. One of its most notable monuments, the stone cross in Ruthwell Kirk, of *c*. 730, has carved on it a few lines from a Northern Anglo-Saxon poem, *The Dream of the Rood*, the earliest tangible record of what this book is all about, the Scots language.

The old British language, which survives in modern

1

Welsh, gradually died out in Scotland, leaving traces only in place-names like Glasgow, Linlithgow, Leith, Innerleithen, Cumbrae, Montgomery, Traquair, Tranent, Niddrie, Ochiltree, Aberdeen, Aberdour, Abernethy, Aberfeldy. The last four are all north of the Forth-Clyde area where the Picts, a British-speaking people, had held Romans and Angles at bay since the first century. But by the mid-ninth century the Picts had been absorbed by another set of invaders—the Scots. They came over from Ireland and settled first in Argyll (c. 500) and spoke a q-Celtic tongue—called Gaelic in Ireland and Scotland—which became the language of the united Picto-Scottish kingdom of Alba, or Scotland.

Just before 800 a new element appears with Viking invasions sweeping across the north and east of England, and the north and west of Scotland and Ireland. The Scandinavians naturally had a great influence on the language of the territory they occupied, all the more so since they spoke a Norse tongue, a descendant of the Teutonic speech from which Anglo-Saxon was also derived, so that the two languages were cousins so to speak, and without much difficulty intelligible to each other. Northern Anglo-Saxon became permeated with Scandinavian words and forms which ultimately found their way into Scotland. In political terms the influence of the Norsemen was even greater by making it impossible for the kingdom of England to hold on to its dependencies north of the Cheviots, and these were ceded to the kings of Alba, first Strathclyde and then Lothian, in the tenth century. By 1000, then, the linguistic situation was that Scotland had two main languages—Gaelic over most of the country and Anglo-Saxon in the south-east—with Norwegian in Shetland, Orkney and Caithness, brought there by the Vikings; modern place-names in Scotland, of which by far the majority are of Gaelic origin, fairly accurately confirm that pattern.

The vital event which changed all this was the Norman conquest of England when French-speaking Normans, originally Scandinavians, overran England and brought the feudal system with them. In due course some of these arrived at the Scottish court of Malcolm Canmore and his English queen, Margaret. They and their three sons, who succeeded them on the throne, and who all had, significantly, English names, made grants of lands all over the Lowlands to those Normans—the Baliols, Bruces, Comyns, and so on—of later Scottish history, and to churchmen and religious orders from England who thereupon brought their households, their land-stewards and bailiffs, their chaplains and major-domos, cooks, bottle-washers and hangers-on, to help them to run their new estates. And while the barons themselves may have spoken French, most of their retinue spoke Anglo-Saxon, or rather that increasingly mixed speech which was still mainly Anglic in grammar but had a large and growing accretion of French vocabulary, and so was really Anglo-French, though it kept its national name 'English' or, as they pronounced it in Scotland, 'Inglis'.

With the extension of the feudal system over the fertile areas of Scotland north and south, the speech of Lothian spread in step, pushing Gaelic into the hills in Galloway, where it died out in the seventeenth century, and into the Highlands. The geographical border between Highlands and Lowlands corresponds roughly to the linguistic boundary between Gaelic and Scots, a line running in a great eastward crescent from Nairn to Dunkeld and then south-westward to Aberfoyle and the Gareloch. Beyond this Highland line Gaelic was spoken until the eighteenth century, when after the Jacobite risings of 1715 and 1745, the Highlands were opened up by military occupation. By then English had become the standard official language of the whole United Kingdom, and so when the Highlander ultimately abandoned his Gaelic, he replaced it with Highland English. His ancestors had never spoken Scots.

By 1200 English farm names and personal names were springing up as far as the north-east. Another important factor in the anglicisation process was the establishment of burghs for the encouragement of trade and industry. Again English names are prominent among the early lists of burgesses, even in Inverness; and, incidentally, the burghs provided a home for many craftsmen, especially weavers, who were encouraged to come from the Netherlands to practise their skills, and whose native language was Flemish.

The great prop of feudalism was the charter, which was as statistics is to the modern bureaucrat, and some of these charters have survived from the twelfth century, all in Latin, the official chancery language of the kingdom, but as time goes on containing more and more vernacular glosses where the Latin needed explaining. Unlike England where French remained in use among the magnates and for state and legal purposes, it fell into disuse in Scotland early in the fourteenth century and 'Inglis' superseded it as the language for correspondence. Now Inglis appears as the vehicle of literature as well—in Barbour's *Brus*, 1375, and in translations of Latin and French poems, no longer intelligible in their original to the literate classes who wished to read them. In 1398 the Scottish Parliament began to enact its statutes in the vernacular instead of in Latin.

Meanwhile the dialects of Anglo-Saxon south of the Humber had developed along their own lines. For obvious political reasons the speech of London, the capital, came to the fore and this, together with the importance of the Universities of Oxford and Cambridge and the works of poets like Chaucer, resulted in the dialect of the English home counties developing into the official national language of England, and in the other dialects, including the Northern, ceasing to be used for official or literary purposes after 1450. In Scotland, however, the Northern dialect with its strong Scandinavian colouring, especially that spoken in the Forth area, became the official speech of the kingdom of Scotland, the King of Scotland's Scots as opposed to the King of England's English. In the poetry of Henryson, Dunbar, Douglas, Lyndsay and others, it was used for a literature of considerable bulk and distinction, and by 1450 it had begun to assume the classical form of an all-purpose language. Gavin Douglas indeed used it for a verse translation of the *Aeneid* and describes his difficulties in making it adequate to render Virgil's diction, chiefly in vocabulary, which he remedied, as all languages do, by borrowing from others.

Writers, however, began to be conscious of the differences between the speech of the north and the speech of the south, and to mark its now independent national status it was renamed 'Scottis' in place of 'Inglis', though the older term survived alongside the new for a considerable time.

The sixteenth century can be considered the high-water mark of the Scots language. While the first half saw it growing to its full status as a national speech adequate for all the demands laid on it, for poetry, for literary and official prose, public records and the ordinary business transactions of life, the second half felt the first of the great blows which halted its growth and ultimately led to its replacement by English.

In 1560 the Reformation took place in Scotland and the English Bible, translated in that same year by English refugees in Geneva, was, in default of a Scots translation which never existed, circulated throughout the land. Its language became familiar to the people as the language of solemnity and abstract thought, of theological and philosophical disputation, while Scots remained as the language of ordinary life, of the domestic, sentimental and comic, and from here we can trace the split mind that Scots have had about their native language ever since. A classic example is Burns's *The Cotter's Saturday Night*, where the domestic scene is described in Scots, but as soon as the big ha' Bible is brought out the poem glides into English by the association of the Bible with the English language, which had gained spiritual prestige through the Reformation.

The next blow came in 1603 with the Union of the Crowns when the Court and a number of literary men as well as politicians who frequented it moved to London and adopted the speech of their new surroundings. The Scottish poets of the early seventeenth century, including the king himself, Drummond and Alexander, took to writing English, and there followed a fairly speedy anglicisation of the social classes who commuted between Scotland and London. Government from London also led to increasing anglicising of

Scottish official documents and records, both central and local, private as well as public, as correspondence between the two capitals grew. English now acquired a social prestige in Scotland which it has maintained in increasing measure ever since.

The last and conclusive blow to Scots was the Union of the Parliaments in 1707 when the legislature was transferred to London, and hence forward the official *written* language of the whole country was that of the legislative capital. The King's English had displaced the King's Scots and added political prestige to itself.

The *spoken* language of course remained either full Scots or half and half according to the informality of the subject or the social status of the speaker; and even when ostensibly English in grammar and vocabulary, the pronunciation and intonation would be Scots. Scots M.Ps faced this problem in the new British Parliament and by 1761 were taking lessons in elocution for the elimination of provincial accents, when an Irishman came to Edinburgh to teach the local bigwigs to speak English.

But there was a literary and linguistic reaction, led in the 1720s by the writer Allan Ramsay who republished the best of Scottish medieval poetry and used Scots for his own poems and his play, *The Gentle Shepherd*. He showed just how much the Scots tongue was still capable of and paved the way for his successors, Fergusson and, above all, Burns. This was, however, only a half restoration of Scots. It was restricted to poetry and there, too, to subjects of an emotional, domestic or jocular nature. There was no epic, metaphysical or philosophical poetry, and Scots for the full and general purposes of prose has never been attempted since 1700 except as an occasional *tour de force*. Official formal prose had gone over to English. Literary prose, such as exists, is on the same restricted scale as the poetry after 1700; it is found only in the dialogue of novels, as in Scott, who employs it for characters in a status of life where Scots would still normally have been spoken in the eighteenth century—by farmers, fishermen, old ladies, gardeners, even Glasgow bailies, servant maids,

6

old soldiers and beggars—and within these limits Scott uses it extremely well, carefully shading the Scots according to the rank, sex, profession and so on, of the speaker, so that even within the narrowing limits of colloquial Scots dialogue, the speech has a considerable variation of style. Scott's own narrative, however, is entirely in English and this applies to nearly all Scottish novelists since: Hogg, Susan Ferrier, George MacDonald, Stevenson, Barrie, George Douglas Brown, Neil Munro and the moderns. One exception is Galt, who experimented with a kind of Scotticised English in the narrative of his novels; another is Lewis Grassic Gibbon, who wrote his *Scots Quair* (1932-4) in an English full of Scottish idioms and rhythms. The very fact that he did so shows that the problem of the language of Scottish literature has not yet been solved despite the omnipresence of English.

A standard language is of necessity a somewhat artificial construct, because one of its functions is to serve for writing, which lacks the spontaneity and looseness of ordinary speech and demands an exactness and consistency not to be expected in conversation.

There must always have been local dialects of spoken Scots from the earliest period. There are traces of these in written sources from the late fifteenth century, but dialect literature proper begins in Scotland in the eighteenth century when Scots had given place to English as the national language, and in the absence of a standard to which writers and literate speakers can adhere, each one can speak only as best he can in conformity with the conventions of his own locality—his own native dialect in fact. As the national language fades out, a series of dialects supersedes it all over Scotland, all of them now under heavy pressure from the English of the school, Press, radio and television, slipping down the social scale and in a state of attrition, as we shall see. Not only so, but disintegrating as they are, they have come to colour more and more such literary Scots as is still written. Whether a Scots literature, as opposed to a Scots dialect literature, exists any more, is a fine point that we shall return to later.

7

What Does It Look Like?

To answer this question we must look at a selection of passages from Scottish writing as they occur in chronological sequence throughout the centuries, beginning with an extract from Barbour's *Brus*, written in 1375 but preserved only in MSS. of a hundred years later. The passage from Book X, v. 584, describes the stratagem to capture Edinburgh Castle in 1313. Have a go at it and see how much you can make out without help from the glossary. One of the trickiest bits is to master the spelling. It helps to know that *i* and *y* are used fairly indiscriminately, as in *hym*, *nycht*, *clymbyng*, *syt*; *purvait* is purveyed; *thai* is they; *v* and *w* also interchange as in *vay*; *quh* is equivalent to English *wh*. Otherwise it is chiefly a matter of getting to know the meanings of the queer words, like *abaid*, delay, abiding, and as a verb, tarried; *wicht*, valiant; *assay*, attempt; *gat*, road; *schore*, precipitous; *tofruschit*, smashed to pieces; *aynd*, breath. Notice also how some of the words differ from the corresponding English ones, especially in their vowels; thus *soyne* is English *soon*, but the *oy* stands for a pronunciation like the *eu* in French *feu*; *mair* is more; *braid*, broad; *swa*, so; *ta*, take; *tane*, taken; *let* is to prevent.

> 'Soyne eftir wes the leddir maid,
> And than the erll, but mair abaid,
> Purvait hym on a nycht prevaly,
> With thritty men, wicht and hardy,
> And in ane myrk nycht held thar vay.
> Thai put thame in full hard assay,
> And to gret perell sekyrly.
> I trow, mycht thai haf seyne cleirly,
> That gat had nocht beyn undirtane,
> Thouch thai to let thame had nocht ane.
> For the crag wes hye and hydwous,

And the clymbyng rycht perelus.
For hapnyt ony to slyde or fall,
He suld be soyne tofruschit all.
The nycht wes myrk, as I herd say,
And till the fut soyne cummyn ar thai
Of the crag, that wes hye and schore,
Than Williame Francous thame befor
Clam in the crykis forouth thaim ay,
And at the bak him followit thai,
With mekill payne, quhill to, quhill fra;
Thai clam into the crykis swa,
Quhill half the craggis thai clummyn had;
And thair ane place thai fand so braid,
That thai mycht syt on anerly.
And thai were ayndles and wery,
And thair abaid thair aynd to ta.'

The next passage is from a letter of 1400 written by the Earl of March to Henry IV of England asking for his help against the Earl's own sovereign, Robert III, whose son had jilted the Earl's daughter. The style, while somewhat formal, illustrates how the nobility actually spoke. Observe a certain French flavour about the style and vocabulary, as well as the signature and address, although the Earl calls his language 'englis' and disclaims facility in French. But his wife wrote to Henry in French. Henry, incidentally, was the first Norman king of England to speak English.

Again *u*, *v* and *w*, and *i* and *y* interchange; *yh* represents *y*; *dedeyn*, deign; *quhill*, till; *likis*, seems good to; *myster*, need; *feirde*, fourth; *suppowell*, support; *defowle*, insult.

'Alsa, noble Prynce, will yhe dedeyn to graunt and to send me yhour saufconduyt, endurand quhill the fest of the natiuite of Seint John the Baptist fore a hundreth knichtis and squiers and seruantz gudes hors and hernais als wele within wallit town as with owt or in qwat other resonable manere that yhow likis fore trauaillyng and dwellyng within yhour land gif I hafe myster. And, excellent Prynce, syn that I clayme to be of kyn tyll

9

yhow and it peraventour nocht knawen on yhour parte I
schew it to yhour lordschip be this my lettre that gif
dame Alice the Bewmount was yhour graunde dame,
dame Mariory Comyne hyrre full sister was my graunde
dame on the tother syde, sa that I am bot of the feirde
degre of kyn tyll yhow the quhilk in alde tyme was callit
neire and syn I am in swilk degre till yhow I requere
yhow as be way of tendirness thareof and for my seruice
in maner as I haue before writyn, that yhe will vou-
chesauf tyll help me and suppowell me tyll gete
amendes of the wrangis and the defowle that ys done
me, sendand tyll me gif yhow likis yhour answere of this
with all gudely haste. And, noble Prynce, mervaile yhe
nocht that I write my lettres in englis for that ys mare
clere to myne vnderstandyng than latyne or Fraunche.
Excellent mychty and noble Prynce, the haly Trinite
hafe yhow evermare in kepyng. Writyn at my castell of
Dunbarr the xviij day of Feuerer. Le Count de la
Marche Descoce. Au tresexcellent trespuissant et tres-
noble Prince le Roy Dengleterre.'

We now turn to a different kind of Scots, fashionable for
sophisticated Court poetry in the later fifteenth century and
imitated directly from French originals and indirectly from
the imitator, Chaucer. The language, as a result, is more like
English, and there are frequently English forms like *quhois,
go, moir, so, most,* where Scots would have said *quhais, gae,
mair, sae, maist.* The *ll* remains in *full* and *all,* although
Dunbar himself would have said *fu* and *aa.* As a result an *l*
appears in *awalk* (awake) to indicate a long vowel, although it
has no etymological business to be there. Another feature is
the number of words of French or Latin origin, like *depaynt*
(French *dépeint,* depicted), *benyng, ring* (*ng* representing the
French sound *gne*), *mansuetude* (gentleness), *illumynit, atteir,
curage, plane* (from *plaindre,* to lament), *promyt* (*promettre,*
promise), *discryve, plesance, annamyllit, gent, dulce, redolent.*
In the last line *doing fleit* is a Scots poetic way of saying simply
'floating, dripping'.

10

The general style is ornamental (it was known as 'aureate' or gilded) with words chosen to convey brilliance of sound and light. The passage is from Dunbar's allegory *The Thrissill and the Rose*, written in honour of the marriage of James IV to Margaret, sister of Henry VIII, in 1503.

'Me thocht fresche May befoir my bed upstude
In weid depaynt of mony divers hew,
Sobir, benyng, and full of mansuetude,
In brycht atteir of flouris forgit new,
Hevinly of color, quhyt, reid, broun, and blew,
Balmit in dew and gilt with Phebus bemys,
Quhill all the hous illumynit of hir lemys.

Slugird, scho said, awalk annone for schame,
And in my honour sum thing thow go wryt,
The lork hes done the mirry day proclame,
To rais up luvaris with confort and delyt.
Yit nocht incresis thy curage to indyt,
Quhois hairt sum tyme hes glaid and blisfull bene,
Sangis to mak undir the levis grene.

Quhairto, quod I, sall I uprys at morrow,
For in this May few birdis hard I sing?
Thai haif moir caus to weip and plane thair sorrow,
Thy air it is nocht holsum nor benyng;
Lord Eolus dois in thy sessone ring;
So busteous ar the blastis of his horne,
Amang thy bewis to walk I haif forborne.

With that this lady sobirly did smyll,
And said, Uprys, and do thy observance;
Thow did promyt, in Mayis lusty quhyle,
For to discryve the Ros of most plesance.
Go se the birdis how they sing and dance,
Illumynit our with orient skyis brycht,
Annamyllit richely with new asur lycht.

Quhen this was said, depairtit scho, this quene,
And enterit in a lusty gairding gent
And than, me thocht, full hastely besene,
In serk and mantill eftir hir I went
Into this garth, most dulce and redolent
Off herb and flour and tendir plantis sueit,
And grene levis doing of dew doun fleit.'

Lemis, rays; *busteous*, violent; *bewis*, boughs; *gent*, fair;
besene, arrayed; *serk*, shirt; *garth*, garden.

In quite different style is the comic poem, 'The Wyf of
Auchtermuchty', ascribed to one Moffat and written, pre-
sumably in Fife, in the first half of the sixteenth century. It is
based on the folk motif of a lazy peasant and his wife who
exchanged roles for a day and of the husband's disasters with
housekeeping. The husband starts the argument:

'Quoth he, Quhair is my horsis corne?
My ox has neither hay nor stray.
Dame, ye mon to the pluch to morne;
I salbe hussy gif I may.
Husband, quod scho, Content am I
To tak the pluche my day abowt
Sa ye will rowll baith kavis and ky
And all the house baith in and owt.

Bot sen that ye will husy skep ken,
First ye sall sift and syne sall kned,
And ay as ye gang but and ben,
Luk that the bairnis dryt not the bed.
Yeis lay a soft wisp to the kill;
We haif ane deir ferme on our heid.
And ay as ye gang furth and in,
Keip weill the gaslingis frae the gled.

The wyf was up richt lait at evin,—
I pray God gif hir evill to fair—

Scho kyrnd the kyrne and skwmd it clene,
And left the gudman bot the bledoch bair.
Than in the mornyng up scho gatt
And on hir hairt laid hir disiwne;
Scho put alsmekle in hir lap
As micht haif serd thame baith at nwne.

Sayis, Jok, will thow be maistir of wark?
And thow sall had and I sall kall.
Is promeis the ane gud new sark,
Athir of round claith or of small.
Scho lowsit oxin aucht or nyne,
And hynt ane gadstaff in hir hand;
And the gudman rais eftir syne
And saw the wyf had done command.

And cavd the gaislingis fwrth to feid—
Thair was bot sevinsum of thame all—
And by thair cumis the gredy gled
And likkit up fyve, left him bot twa.
Than owt he ran in all his mane
Howsone he hard the gaislings cry,
Bot than or he come in agane
The calfis brak lows and sowkit the ky.

The calvis and ky being met in the lone
The man ran with a rung to red,
Than by thair cumis ane ill willy cow
And brodit his buttok quhill that it bled.
Than hame he ran to ane rok of tow
And he satt doun to say the spynning.
I trow he lowtit our neir the low;
Quod he, This wark has ill begynning.'

The contrast in vocabulary with the Dunbar passage is
marked. Latinate words are almost entirely absent; the
others are ordinary vernacular: *ky, but and ben, dryt, gasling,
kyrne,* etc. This colloquial style is also seen in the shortened

13

forms of words, *hussy* for *housewife*; *sen* for *since*; *Is, yeis* for *I sall, ye sall*; *serd* for *served*; *cavd* for *called* (drove); *evin*, despite the spelling, is pronounced *een*, as the metre and rhyme with *clene* show. Somewhat similarly, *evil* was often written where the etymologically distinct *ill* was intended; *mon* is now written *maun*, must; *rowll*, rule; *hussyskep* is housewifery, *-skep* being the northern form of the common English suffix *-ship*; *but and ben*, from one end of the house to the other; *dryt* is to soil with excrement, the original form and meaning of English *dirt*; *kill*, kiln, still so pronounced in Scotland; *bledoch* is Gaelic *blàthach*, buttermilk; *disiwne*, breakfast; *hairt*, in the colloquial sense of stomach; *gadstaff*, goad; *sevinsum*, seven in all, cf. *foursome*, *eightsome*. Notice how the married pair address one another as *ye* but the servant Jock is addressed as *thow*; *lone*, grass-track; *rung*, stick; *redd*, separate; *brod*, jab; *rok*, distaff; *say*, try; *lowtit*, stooped; *our*, too; *low*, fire.

We are now at the event which did so much to alter the course of the Scots language, the Reformation, and the man who did most to bring it about, John Knox. Knox spent ten years in England and with English speakers abroad, and it was a taunt of his Catholic opponents that he had forgotten 'our auld plane Scottis, quhilk your mother lerit you'. Certainly he (or a secretary who wrote at his dictation) used many English forms in his writing, though no doubt his speech was Scots enough, especially after he returned to Edinburgh. In the following passage from his *History of the Reformation in Scotland*, Book III, we can see the influence of English at work:

'The storm which had continuit neire the space of a moneth, brak in the verry tyme of thair reteiring, quhair mony thocht thei sould have beein stayit, till that reasonabill cumpanie mycht have bein assemblit to have fouchtein thame; and for that purpois did Wilyeaume Kirkcaldy cut the Brig of Toullibody. But the Frenche, expert aneuch in suche facts, tuik doun the roofe of a parish kirk, and maid a brig over the same watter, called

Dovane; and so thai eschapit, and come to Striveling, and syne to Leith. Yit in thair retourning thai lost dyverse; amongis quhome thair was one quhois miserable end we man rehers. As the French spoilyied the countrye in thair retourning, one capitaine or soldiour, we cannot tell, bot he had a reid cloik and a gilt morrion, entered upon a poore woman, that dwelt in the Whytsyd, and began to spoyle. The poore woman offered unto him suche breid as sche had reddy prepared. But he, in no wayis thairwith content, wald have the meill and a lytill salt beiff which the poore woman had to susteine hir awin lyfe, and the lyves of hir poore chylderein; neather could tearis, nor pitifull wourdis, mittigat the merciles man, but he wald have quhatsoever he mycht carie. The poore woman perceiving him so bent, and that he stoupped doun in hir tub, for the taking foorth of suche stufe as was within it, first cowped up his heillis, so that his heid went doun; and thairefter, outher by hirself, or if ony uther cumpanie come to help hir, but thair he endid his unhappie lyfe; God so punissing his crewell hairt, quho could nocht spair a misserable woman in that extremetie.'

There is nothing particularly Scots about the vocabulary except *syne*, then, thereafter; *man*, must; and *cowp* for overturn, still in common use. Scots forms like *brak, mony, mycht, brig, reid, wald, awin, heid, doun, nocht, efter*, mingle with English forms like *quhome, quhois, quho, one, so, sche,* such, which, and, similarly, Scots and English spellings appear indiscriminately even in the same word, as *quh-* and *wh-*; *purpois, twik,* but *roof, poore; aneuch, maid, thai, amongis, spoilyie,* but *spoyl; bot* but *but; neir,* but *tears; -ed* and *-it* for the ending of the past tense and so on.

The mixed style we have seen in Knox grows more marked in the course of the next century and the distance between formal and colloquial speech continues to widen. In the following passage from a witch trial of the mid-seventeenth century we have the official record by the clerk of the court

15

and the depositions of the accused woman. She undoubtedly spoke her native Moray Scots which has been somewhat modified as it was rendered in the legal and anglicised style of the notary.

The text is from R. Pitcairn, *Criminal Trials in Scotland* (1833), III, Appendix No. vii; the date is 1662 and the place Auldearn.

'The quhilk day, in presence of me, Johne Innes, Notar Publict, and witnessis abownamet, all under-subscrywand, the said Issobell Gowdie, appeiring pene-tent for hir haynous sinnes of Witchcraft, and that sho haid bein ower lang in that service; without ony com-pulsitouris, proceidit in hir confessione, in manner efter following, to wit: As I was goeing betwix the townes of Drumdewin and the Headis, I met with the Divell, and ther covenanted in a maner with him; and I promeisit to meit him in the night time in the Kirk of Aulderne, quhilk I did. And the first thing I did ther that night, I denyed my baptisme, and did put the one of my handis to the crowne of my head and the uther to the sole of my foot, and then renouncet all betwixt my two hands ower to the Divell. He was in the Readeris dask, and a black book in his hand. Margret Brodie, in Aulderne, held me up to the Divell to be baptised be him; and he marked me in the showlder, and suked owt my blood at that mark, and spowted it in his hand, and sprinkling it on my hand, said, "I baptise the Janet, in my awin name!" And within a quhill we all remoowed. Sometymes he haid buitis and sometymes shoes on his foot; but still his foot are forked and cloven. He vold be sometimes with us like a dear, or a rae. Johne Taylor and Janet Bread-head, his wyff, in Belnakeith, Dowglas and I myself, met in the Kirkyaird of Nairne, and we raised an unchristened child owt of its greaff; and at the end of Breadleyis cornfield land, just opposit to the Milne of Nairne, we took the said child, with the naillis of our fingeris and toes, pickles of all sortis of grain, and blaidis of keall, and haked them all verie small, mixed

16

altogither; and did put a pairt thereof among the
mukheapes of Breadleyes landis, and therby took away
the fruit of his cornes, etc.; and we pairted it among two
of our Coevens. Whan we tak cornes at Lambes, we tak
bot abowt two sheawes, whan the cornes ar full; or two
stokis of keall, or therby, and that gives ws the fruit of
the corn land or keall-yaird whair they grew. And it may
be, we will keip yt while Yewll or Pace, and than devyd
it amongst ws. Ther ar threttein persones in my Coven.
Befor Candlmas we went beeast Kinlosse, and ther we
yoaked an plewghe of paddokis. The Divell held the
plewgh, and John Yownge in Mebestowne, our Officer,
did drive the plewgh. Paddokis did draw the plewgh as
oxen; qwickens wer sowmes, a riglens horne wes a
cowter and an piece of an riglens horne wes an sok. We
went two several tymes abowt; and all we of the Coeven
went still wp and downe with the plewghe, prayeing to
the Divell for the fruit of that land, and that thistles and
briers might grow ther.'

Again Scots and English forms are mixed up in the -t and
-d endings of past tense and participles, quh- and wh-; -and is
being supplanted by -ing in present participles, subscryvand,
but goeing, following, sprinkling. Spellings are in the main
English, not Scots; so buitis, but foot, book, took, blood;
remoowed; rae (roe), but toe; blaid, pairt, but meall, sheawes,
dear; gh is found throughout for ch, but ei persists in appeir,
meit, keip, threttein. Scots spellings have given way to English
in one, shoes, two, thistles, amongst. Where the Scots survives
is in the vocabulary of the rural world of Isobel Gowdie:
pickle, grain of corn; blaid, leaf; stok, stalk; paddok, frog;
quickens, couch-grass; sowmes, traces; riglen, undeveloped
ram; coven is a company of thirteen into which groups of
witches were organised; compulsitouris, compulsion—by
threats or torture.

We now jump more than a century over the important
period when Scots ceased to be a full language and survived
only partly as a literary vehicle for poetry and as a series of

17

local dialects. But limited as its range was, in the hands of a genius with words, such as Burns, it took on a new lease of life. His outstanding skill was to make ordinary folk speech fit for the nuances of poetic imagination, albeit a limited one, and he is probably at his best in the epistles and addresses composed in the stanza metre so eminently suited to the twists and turns and asides of conversation.

Here he hails Satan himself in the 'Address to the Deil' written about the end of 1784. The only difficulty is in the odd Scots word no longer in use, as *Clootie* (pronounced *Clittie*), a nickname for the Devil as having *cluits* or hooves; *spairges*, splashes; *cootie*, a way of spelling *kittie*, a little tub or bucket; *scaud*, scald; *lowan heugh*, flaming pit; *lag*, slow, dilatory; *blate*, shy; *scaur*, scary, timid; *tirlan*, stripping, unroofing; *eldritch*, elfish, unearthly; *douse*, gentle; *boortries*, bower-trees, elder-bushes; *sklentan*, slanting; *rash-buss*, clump of rushes; *nieve*, fist; *stoor*, raucous.

'O Thou! whatever title suit thee—
Auld Hornie, Satan, Nick or Clootie,
Wha in yon cavern grim and sootie,
    Clos'd under hatches,
Spairges about the brunstane cootie
    To scaud poor wretches.

Hear me, Auld Hangie, for a wee,
An' let poor damnèd bodies be;
I'm sure sma' pleasure it can gie,
    E'en to a deil,
To skelp an' scaud poor dogs like me
    An' hear us squeel!

Great is thy pow'r an' great thy fame;
Far kenn'd an' noted is thy name;
An' tho' yon lowan heugh's thy hame
    Thou travels far;
An' faith! thou's neither lag, nor lame,
    Nor blate, nor scaur.

Whyles, ranging like a roaran lion,
For prey, a' holes an' corners tryin:
Whyles, on the strong-wing'd tempest flyin,
  Tirlan the kirks;
Whyles, in the human bosom pryin,
  Unseen thou lurks.

I've heard my rev'rend graunie say,
In lanely glens ye like to stray;
Or where auld, ruin'd castles, gray,
  Nod to the moon,
Ye fright the nightly wand'rer's way,
  Wi' eldritch croon.

When twilight did my graunie summon,
To say her pray'rs, douse, honest woman!
Aft 'yont the dyke she's heard you bumman,
  Wi' eerie drone;
Or, rustling, thro' the boortries coman,
  Wi' heavy groan.

Ae dreary, windy, winter night,
The stars shot down wi' sklentan light,
Wi' you, mysel, I gat a fright,
  Ayont the lough;
Ye, like a rash-buss, stood in sight,
  Wi' waving sugh.

The cudgel in my nieve did shake,
Each bristl'd hair stood like a stake,
When wi' an eldritch stoor "quaick, quaick",
  Amang the springs,
Awa ye squatter'd like a drake,
  On whistling wings. . . .'

The marriage of sense, sound and atmosphere in the last
three stanzas is quite remarkable.

19

Scott in negotiating with Ballantyne for the publishing of his first novel *Waverley* said, 'Burns by his poetry has already attracted attention to everything Scottish and I confess I can't see why I should not be able to keep the flame alive, merely because I write Scotch in prose and he wrote it in rhyme'; and wherever it was appropriate he used Scots for the dialogue of his characters with remarkable richness and accuracy. He obviously strives to get the maximum 'Scottish' effect by the use of idiomatic phrases, proverbs, historical terms and so on. Here in *Rob Roy*, Chapter xxii, he conveys in short compass the social and political attitudes of the Highlands in the early eighteenth century and the Lowlander's reactions, half critical, half sympathetic, to his compatriot from the hills.

"Ye're a bauld desperate villain, sir," retorted the undaunted Bailie, "and ye ken that I ken ye to be sae, and that I wadna stand a moment for my ain risk."

"I ken weel," said the other, "ye hae gentle bluid in your veins, and I wad be laith to hurt my ain kinsman. But I'll gang out here as free as I came in, or the very wa's o' Glasgow Tolbooth shall tell o't these ten years to come."

"Weel, weel," said Mr Jarvie, "bluid's thicker than water; and it liesna in kith, kin, and ally, to see motes in ilk other's een if other een see them no. It wad be sair news to the auld wife below the Ben of Stuckavrallachan, that you, ye Hieland limmer, had knockit out my harns, or that I had kilted you up in a tow. But ye'll own, ye dour deevil, that were it no your very sell, I wad hae grippit the best man in the Hielands."

"Ye wad hae tried, cousin," answered my guide, "that I wot weel; but I doubt ye wad hae come aff wi' the short measure; for we gang-there-out Hieland bodies are an unchancy generation when you speak to us o' bondage. We downa bide the coercion of gude braidclaith about our hinderlans; let a be breeks o' freestone, and garters o' iron."

20

"Ye'll find the stane breeks and the airn garters, ay, and the hemp cravat, for a' that, neighbour," replied the Bailie. "Nae man in a civilized country ever played the pliskies ye hae done—but e'en pickle in your ain pock-neuk—I hae gi'en ye warning."

"Well, cousin," said the other, "ye'll wear black at my burial?"

"Deil a black cloak will be there, Robin, but the corbies and the hoodie-craws, I'se gie ye my hand on that. But whar's the gude thousand pund Scots that I lent ye, man, and when am I to see it again?"

"Where it is," replied my guide, after the affectation of considering for a moment, "I cannot justly tell—probably where last year's snaw is."

"And that's on the tap of Schehallion, ye Hieland dog," said Mr Jarvie, "and I look for payment frae you where ye stand."

"Ay," replied the Highlander, "but I keep neither snaw nor dollars in my sporran. And as to when you'll see it—why, just when the king enjoys his ain again, as the auld sang says."

"Warst of a', Robin," retorted the Glaswegian, "—I mean, ye disloyal traitor—warst of a'! Wad ye bring popery in on us, and arbitrary power, and a foist and a warming-pan, and the set forms, and the curates, and the auld enormities o' surplices and cearments? Ye had better stick to your auld trade o' theft-boot, blackmail, spreaghs, and gillravaging—better stealing nowte than ruining nations."

Bauld, bold; *laith,* loath; *een,* eyes; *limmer,* rascal; *harns,* brains; *kilted,* trussed, tucked; *grippit,* seized; *wi' the short measure,* second-best; *gang-there-out,* roaming, wandering; *downa,* are unable to; *hinderlans,* behinds; *let a be,* let alone; *pliskie,* prank; *pickle in your ain pock-neuk,* a Scots proverb, 'look to yourself, take your own responsibility'; *corbie,* raven. The last paragraph alludes to the Presbyterian and Whig attitudes to Episcopacy and Jacobitism. *Theft-boot,* taking a bribe from a thief to conceal his crime; *blackmail*, originally an illegal levy imposed by Highland rustlers on Lowland farmers to obtain immunity from plunder; *spreagh*, cattle raid; *gillravaging*, riotous living, rampaging; *nowte*, cattle. The phrase originated in a taunt by Patrick Ogilvie, who was a cattle dealer, against his brother, the Earl of Seafield, who engineered the Union of 1707.

The problem of retaining, or perhaps more correctly restoring, 'Scottishness' to prose was tackled in a rather different way by Scott's contemporary, John Galt, who tries to infuse Scottish words and idioms into the narrative as well as the dialogue of his novels, giving added verisimilitude to this by the fiction that the whole story is being told by some old-fashioned person who would retain more Scots in his speech than an up-and-coming author. In the following passage from *The Annals of the Parish* (1821), Chapter xvii, the words purport to come from the reminiscences of the aged parish minister speaking a mixture of mid-eighteenth-century Scots and the English expected from his position:

'The listing was a catching distemper. Before the summer was over, the other three of the farming lads went off with the drum, and there was a wailing in the parish, which made me preach a touching discourse. I likened the parish to a widow woman with a small family, sitting in her cottage by the fireside, herself spinning with an eident wheel, ettling her best to get them a bit and a brat, and the poor weans all canty about the hearthstane—the little ones at their playocks, and the elder at their tasks—the callans working with hooks and lines to catch them a meal of fish in the morning— and the feckless wee bairns laid on the bed of sickness, and their forlorn mother sitting by herself at the embers of a cauldrife fire; her tow done, and no a bodle to buy more; drooping a silent and salt tear for her babies, and thinking of days that war gone, and like Rachel weeping for her children, she would not be comforted. . . .

22

They both told me that they had never heard such a good discourse but I do not think they were great judges of preachings. How indeed could Mr Howard know anything of sound doctrine, being educated, as he told me, at Eton school, a prelatic establishment? Nevertheless, he was a fine lad; and though a little given to frolic and diversion, he had a principle of integrity, that afterwards kythed into much virtue; for during this visit he took a notion of Effie Malcolm, and the lassie of him, then a sprightly and blooming creature, fair to look upon, and blithe to see.'

The Scotticisms are subtly worked into the structure, e.g. *listing*, still the current Scots form for English *enlisting*; *small family*, the Scots idiom for a family of young (*not* few) children; *eident*, industrious, busy; *ettle*, a favourite word of Galt, to strive, aim, attempt; *brat*, a piece of cloth, clothing; *wean* (for *wee ane*), little one; *canty*, merry; *playock* (diminutive form of *play*), a toy; *callan*, common in Renfrewshire and Ayrshire, a lad, boy; *cauldrife*, chilly; *war* for *were*; *kythe*, to appear, make itself known, show itself.

Later prose writers tended to follow Scott's method in their use of Scots and there are good passages in Stevenson, e.g. 'Thrawn Janet' or 'The Tale of Tod Lapraik' in *Catriona*, in Barrie's *A Window in Thrums*, or George Douglas Brown's *The House with the Green Shutters*, or in Ian MacLaren, S. R. Crockett, Neil Munro, John Buchan, Fionn MacColla. But the line tried out by Galt was continued by D. M. Moir, Mrs Oliphant and some minor writers, and the whole question was reopened by the 'Lallans' movement and a new approach made by Lewis Grassic Gibbon in his *Scots Quair*, as described in the last chapter.

How Does It Sound?

Of necessity this chapter will have to be rather technical and some of the detail can be skipped by the general reader, but it could be a help to the student to begin with a few notes on the phonetic symbols used to represent the pronunciation of the words discussed. The symbols follow the International Phonetic Alphabet and are indicated between / /.

The vowels have their Continental qualities: /a/ as in *man*, /ɑ/ as in *charm*, /ɛ/ as in *men*, /e/ as in *main*, /i/ as in *mean*, /ɪ/ as in *mint*, /o/ as in *moan*, /ɔ/ as in *mont*, /u/ as in *moon*, /ə/ as the *a* in *woman*. The sound heard in standard English *good*, *put*, is no longer in use in Scots. Scots also has the sounds /ø/ as in French *peu*, and /y/ as in French *lune*, and the diphthongs /ɑ̈ɪ/ as in *fire*, and /əi/ as in *bite*, /ʌu/ as in *now*, and /ɔi/ as in *boy*. Anglo-Saxon long vowels are written with a stroke above them.

Most of the consonant symbols explain themselves, but /ʒ/ is the *z* sound in *azure*; /ð/ is *th* in *this*, /θ/ the *th* in *thin*; /ʃ/ is *sh*, /ŋ/ the *ng* in *sing*; /j/ is *y* in *you*. Scots differs from English in pronouncing the *h* in *wh-* /ʍ/, instead of English /w/; and has in addition the fricative sounds /ç/ as in German *ich*, and /x/ as in German *lach*.

The answer to the question in our title is complicated by the fact that the pronunciation has changed over the centuries, especially in the fifteenth century, and with this came also changes in spelling, further complicated by French usages superimposed on Anglo-Saxon orthography. The earliest Scots spelling is relatively simple and consistent. The vowels were either short or long (indicated in the International Phonetic Alphabet with (long) or without (short) the sign : after the vowel), following the Anglo-Saxon pattern, except that about 1300 long *o* had developed in Northern England and Scotland into the sound /ø/ or in some dialects /y/. Many words in Anglo-Saxon were of two syllables, one

24

accented, the vowel of the second becoming in time the sound /ə/, usually written *e*. The accented vowel, if it was not long in origin, or before two or more consonants, was then lengthened by its position in what is called an open syllable, and the difference between the old short vowel and the old long or lengthened one is still marked in modern English by the survival of *e* in the spelling, though not in the pronunciation of the second syllable. So we differentiate the vowels in *hat* and *hate*, *man* and *mane*, *met* and *mete*, *bit* and *bite*, *hop* and *hope*, *tub* and *tube*. *It will be noticed that in all these the quality of the vowel alters as well as its length (the u of tub is not the same as that of tube)*.

Sometimes both forms might survive and be distinguished in spelling, as *coll* (coal) from Old English *col* along with *cole* from the Old English plural form *colu* with its open syllable. Another change in Scots was that of the unaccented -*e*- in the endings -*es*, -*ed*, -*en*, becoming -*is*, -*it*, -*in*, giving us *horsis*, *mannis*, *muvit*, *stolin*, etc., and this was retained till the late seventeenth century whether the -*i*- was pronounced or not. In ordinary spoken Scots *mannis* would have been pronounced man's as in English, and *stolin* stolen, later stown. Short *i* in an open syllable became long *e*/e:/, and short *u* the long *o* /ø/. So Old Norse *gifa* (give) becomes *geve*, Old English *lifian* (live) becomes *leve*, *lufian* (love) becomes *love* /l v/, and the reader will quickly notice the difference when he compares Modern English *give*, *live*, *widow*, with Scots *gie*, *leeve*, *weeda*.

In the twelfth century the introduction of French spellings brought certain readjustments. The old Anglo-Saxon long *u* was pronounced like French *ou* and hence the spelling *house* for the original *hūs*. But as Scots had developed the sound of French *u* /y/ out of an original long *o*, Anglo-Saxon words with this sound like *gōd* (good), *mōna* (moon), came to be written in Scots after the French fashion, as *gude*, *blude*, *mune*, *dune*, *schule*, *pule*, or *tune*, *sure*, from French itself.

Again the Anglo-Saxon letter ȝ (not to be confused with the phonetic symbol /ʒ/), which had no equivalent in French (it was pronounced according to the succeeding vowel either as

25

g in Dutch *goed* or as *y* in *yes*), disappeared in favour of *gh* or *y* in English but survived till the age of printing in Scotland, along with the sound, later rendered as *ch*. ʒ coalesced with a preceding vowel to form a dipththong, and what had been originally written *a*ʒ, *o*ʒ, *u*ʒ, *æ*ʒ, *e*ʒ, *i*ʒ, now appeared as *aw*, *ow*, *uw*, *ai* or *ay*, *ei* or *ey*, *i(y)*, all diphthongs, both in Scots and English. The persistence of ʒ in Scots till the sixteenth century involved Scottish printers in the difficulty of making do with the nearest corresponding letter in the German type-face, **ʒ**, which was later replaced by the Roman *z*. This resulted in a frequent confusion between ʒ and *z* which appears in spellings of proper names like *Menzies*, *MacKenzie*, *Dalziel*, instead of the correct *Menyies*, *MacKenyie*, *Dalyell*. Indeed the modern pronunciation of *MacKenzie* has been altered to suit the spelling. *Ch* was, however, in English and Scots used to represent the *tsh* sound in words borrowed from French, *chance*, *rich*, *achieve*, *branch*, *preach*, and in Anglo-Saxon words as *church*, *child*, *chicken*, *kitchen*, *speech*, *teach*, and so on, but this has produced ambiguity in Scots with the other *ch* (the *loch* one). Some canny Scots are solving the problem by dropping the second one altogether and going over to the English pronunciation in *light*, *night*, *high*, for *licht*, *nicht*, *heich*, and even, among the most benighted, to *lock* for *loch*.

The first sentence, then, from the passage from Barbour in the previous chapter would have been pronounced something like this:

'Søn 'ɛftɪr wɛs ðə 'ledɪr maːd
and ðan ðə ɛrl but maːr ə'baːd
pur'vɑɪt hɪm ɔn aː nɪçt 'prevali
wɪθ 'θrɛtɪ mɛn wɪçt and har'di
and ɪn a mɪrk nɪçt hɛld ðɑɪr wəi.'

But just after Barbour's time there occurred both in English and Scots a thoroughgoing alteration in the vowel sounds, known as the Great Vowel Shift, which took place over a long time and may well have started much earlier, though the altered vowel sounds do not become unmistakably apparent in rhymes and spellings till after 1400. What happened was that the long vowels started to move from their old positions in the vocal organs and to encroach on their neighbours so that there was a general jostling and shoving, and as one shifted so the others were pushed around in front of it, not unlike the game of musical chairs, or like five marbles in a bowl—move one and the others move too.

The general tendency was to pronounce the vowels higher in the mouth, technically described as 'raising', but they did not go quite the same way in Scots as they did in Southern English. In English long $\bar{a}$ had already moved up the back of the throat to $\bar{o}$, so that Anglo-Saxon *bān* had become *bone*; then the already existing *bone* from Old Norse *bón*, a prayer, was pushed upwards to *u* and so ended in *boon*; but in Scots *bān* went forward as well as upwards to the old *e* /e:/ sound; it was still written with *a* but pronounced *behn* /be:n/; *stān*, stone, gives *stane*; *māra*, more, *mare*; *cāl*, cole, *kale*; *tā*, toe, *tae*; *hāl*, whole; *rād*, a riding, giving English *road*, the highway along which one may ride, and Scots *raid*, a mounted foray, now borrowed into English in this sense of an attack, while Scots has borrowed the English form in the sense of 'way'.

Another long or lengthened front vowel is *e*, of which there were two varieties in Middle English, the one now usually spelt *ee* and at that period pronounced approximately like the *a* in *late*, the other spelt *ea* and pronounced like the *e* in *bet*, and these sounds were kept distinct in English until the eighteenth century. But in Scots they ran together in the sound *ee* /i:/ much earlier, in the sixteenth century, because $\bar{a}$ / :/ in its progress forwards and upwards had pushed original *e* /e:/ in front of it and occupied $\bar{e}$'s old chair, whereas in English $\bar{a}$ had set off in another direction in pursuit of $\bar{o}$. Hence we get the Scots pronunciation *ee* /i:/, usually spelt *ei*, in *reid*, *heid*, *sweit* (sweat), *beir* (bear, carry), *weir* (wear), *teir* (tear, rend), *deif*, *seiven*, *eleiven*, and so on.

The remaining long front vowel *i*, which used to have the sound /i:/, was then faced with pressure from the *es*, pressed in their turn by the *a*s, and being already at the highest frontal point of the mouth, could move no farther in that direction and turned itself from a vowel into the diphthong /əi/ or /aɪ/. This of course happened in English too; but in English also the same process occurred with the long back vowels; the *ā*s became *ō*s, the *ō*s became *ū*s, as in *moon, good, stool*, etc., and *ū* became the diphthong *ow* /ʌu/, sometimes written *ou*, as in *about, foul, sour, mouse*. But because *ā* did not become *ō* in Scots, and *ō* had already become *u, ui* /ø, y/, there was no pressure on *ū*, which remained as before, and hence the Scot still says *oot* /ut/, *hoose* /hus/, *noo* /nu/, *broon* /brun/.

There were already diphthongs arising out of Anglo-Saxon front vowels followed by ȝ, and out of Old French *ai*, and *ei*, as in *day, say, way, rain, grey, clay, pay, pray, plain*. By the late fifteenth century these sounds were pronounced still as diphthongs (like the *i* in *night*) if they were final, i.e. at the very end of a word, but as a simple vowel (like the *e* in *men*) if a consonant or other syllable came after them. Of course many words would produce two sounds, as *day*, singular /daɪ/, but *dayis*, plural /dɛ:z/, *say* /saɪ/, but *sayis* /sɛ:z/. There was ultimately a levelling-out process so that *day, say, gray, pray*, went to /e:/, and *way, clay, pay*, went to /əi/. But the spelling *ai/ay* remained and did duty for both sounds /əi/ and /e/, of which the latter after the vowel shift also represented the original long *a*. This assimilation of *a* and *ai* was helped by a similar change in French where the *ai* diphthong came to be pronounced *e* /ɛ:/ in the twelfth century, though still spelt *ai*. The result was that the *i* in ceasing to have a sound of its own came to be looked on merely as a sign of length in the preceding vowel. This made it possible to introduce a new series of spellings for the vowel system from the fifteenth century onwards. By the end of that century it was possible to find *kale* and *kail*, *sare* and *sair*, *ake* and *aik* (oak), *lafe* and *laif* (loaf).

By the year 1500 the *ai* forms predominate and are the common spellings today. But before the nasals *m* and *n* the tendency was to keep the older spelling, so that we still have

28

hame and not *haim, nane* and not *nain*, and so on. Where the vowel is final in monosyllables, *ae* appears instead, as in *gae, fae* (foe), *wae* (woe).

In a similar way, after 1500, the diphthong *ei/ey* (from an earlier *eʒ*) came to be pronounced /e:/, so that *ē* and *ei* coalesced in sound, but the spelling *ei* takes over from *e*, as in *beit* for *bete* (beat), *speir* for *spere* (a spear or to inquire), *heir* for *here* (hear), *sein* for *sene* (seen), *leid* for *lede* (to lead), *sweir* for *swere* (swear), *breist* for *brest, sleip* for *slepe, seid* for *sede* (seed). It will be noticed that the English equivalents of these are spelt partly with *ea* and partly with *ee*, as originally distinct vowels. In those with *ee* in English, Scots occasionally adopted the spelling *ie*, especially before *r* and *v*, but *ie* for English *ea* is relatively uncommon. In any case, by the second half of the sixteenth century, when the language began to be anglicised, the English spellings *ea* and *ee* gradually introduced themselves, especially in words common to English and Scots, *heat, lead, clean, heal, hear, tree, deal, leap, meat, meal*. Peculiarly Scots words tend to keep the older spelling as *speir* (ask), *meir* (mare), *dreich* (dreary), *bield* (shelter), *neist* (next), but in general the number of alternative spellings increases as the sixteenth and seventeenth centuries proceed.

With the *i* now as a sign of length of vowel, we also find *oi/oy* as a spelling for the sound /o:/ as in *befoir, rois* (rose), *throit, clois*, and when the reader finds them in Middle Scots he must pronounce them just as they are pronounced today in Scottish English; on no account are they to be pronounced as the diphthong *oy* /ɔi/. So in Barbour *soyn* is just a way of spelling *sone*, soon, which later came to be written *sune* and uttered to rhyme with French *lune*. But of course the *oy* /ɔi/ sound *did* exist in Scots in words of French origin, like *joy, annoy, destroy*. Thus *oi* was ambiguous, and again the influence of English, as well as the confusion, led to the abandonment of *oi* for a long *o* in the seventeenth century.

Finally the letter *u* which came to stand in part for the Anglo-Saxon long *o*, also could have *i* stuck on the end of it as a sign of its length, and as a result arises the spelling *ui*, so rare in English, as in *guid, puir, buit, bluid,* for the earlier *gude, pure,* etc. But, as in the case of *ā*, a following nasal seems to have inhibited this spelling, so that *tume, sune, mune,* are preferred to *tuim, suin, muin,* and in monosyllables the *o* usually remained until the nineteenth century, when *ae* replaced it, as in *shae* (shoe), *dae, tae* (to).

Another change in Old Scots involved *l*, which after short back vowels *a, o, u* turned into a *w* sound, often written *u* or even omitted in spelling and later in pronunciation after *a* and *u*. Thus *ba(w)* for ball; *fa(w); ca(w)* for call, drive with shouts, drive in general, hammer in, propel; *saut, maut* (malt), with which one may compare English *calm, half, talk; howe* /hʌu/, hollow; *knowe,* knoll; *fu,* full, drunk; *pu,* pull. The sound *ow* /ʌu/ also developed out of Anglo-Saxon *oȝ*, with resultant ambiguity in such words as *bow,* pronounced like English *bough,* which could mean a boll or measure of grain, or a bow of an archer or fiddler, or an archway, as in the West Bow or the Netherbow in Edinburgh, which the citizens of Scotland's capital persist in mispronouncing 'boh'. To add to the complications, *ow* was often used in older Scots spelling in monosyllables to indicate the sound /u/. Hence *bow* could also be pronounced *boo,* meaning to bow, incline, make an obeisance, bend, and *bowit,* bent, stooping /buːt/. Notice also that Scots and English differ in their treatment of Anglo-Saxon *ow; grow, row* (in a boat), *flow,* have the *oh* sound in English but are diphthongs in Scots, rhyming with *now,* as does the place-name Stow in Midlothian, compared with England's Stow-on-the-Wold, where both nouns have the same vowel sound.

By the seventeenth century, Scots spelling, which 300 years previously had been fairly straightforward, had, through changes in pronunciation and later influence from English spelling, become very erratic. *Ale,* for instance, could be spelt *al(e), ail(l), ayl(l), aell, eall(e), eill,* etc., not to mention another set of variants beginning with *y,* as *yeal, yill* and so on. The verb to *love* appears as *lufe, luf(f), luif(e), lwf(e), luiff, louf(e), lowffe, lofe, loif, luve, lowe, luwe* and later *loe.*

30

The language itself was of course changing throughout this period. The old long and short vowels became confused; most long ones became short but remained long (and short ones acquired length) before certain consonants like *v, z, th* /ð/, and *r,* as in the distinction between the noun *use* (now pronounced *yiss*) and the verb *use (yaize), leaf* and *leave,* the noun *breith* and the verb *breithe.* Short vowels were also lengthened when *l* dropped out after them as in *ba, fa, saut, oo* (wool), or before an original ȝ, as in *say, saw, lay,* etc.

But by the late seventeenth century Scots was being gradually assimilated to English by the loss of vocabulary and the introduction of southern sounds and grammatical forms, often on top of the Scots, so that the regularity of its structure breaks down. In prose writing English was adopted as the standard, but with the literary revival of the early eighteenth century under Allan Ramsay the problem of spelling Scots arose again, and Ramsay's practice has strongly coloured Scots writing ever since. He is far from consistent, showing the usual fluctuation between *ai* and *a* + consonant +*e,* as *sare sair; e(e), ei, ie; i* and *y* for the diphthong; *ou, ow* for the English *oo* and *ow* sounds without distinction, to the confusion of singers and reciters of Scots songs and poems to this day. In words where *l* had dropped off the end, *a* alone is used, but where the *l* was in the middle of a word, Ramsay indicates its place by *u,* as *ba', ca',* but *haud, maut.* He is in fact one of the first writers to use the apostrophe for letters missing in Scots but present in English, no doubt influenced by writing partly for an English market. The English orientation in spelling appears most emphatically in the spellings -*ea*- used as in the corresponding English form, *bread, tear, beard, heart, peat, seat, meal, gleam, beam*; in the spelling -*oo*- for *ui* /y/, as *good* for *guid, stool* for *stuil, boot* for *buit, moon* for *mune, soon* for *sune, nook* for *neuk, shoon* for *shune*; in spelling the past participle in -*ed* instead of the historic and correct -*it*; in representing the guttural -*ch*- by *gh* as in *light, night, sough, laugh,* and the verbal noun and present participle by -*ing,* not differentiating between -*in* and -*an.* Burns does not deviate materially from this; he is fairly consistent in his first edition

31

and in fact introduces his glossary with a short dissertation on pronunciation and spelling. He distinguishes, in theory, the verbal -*an* and -*in*, though he does not always observe this in practice; he anglicises in many words where Scots pronunciation differs from English, as *heart, starve, after, gather, farmer, art* (note, for instance, the spelling and the rhymes in the last verse of 'Ca' the Ewes', *ewes* being Burns's own spelling, though he undoubtedly meant *yowes*).

Scott follows but with much inconsistency, using spellings like *blude, bluid, blood, spear, spier, speir, sa, sae, so*, indiscriminately. Galt, in conformity with his aim to develop a Scottified English style, anglicises even more. By the middle of the nineteenth century with the growth of local dialect writing, some attempt was made to spell more phonetically according to the English system, and *oo* for earlier *ou, ow*, creeps in in *hoose, moose, doon, doot*, and *ee* in *speer, bleeze, reed, deef, freend*, etc., especially in the north-east, where the dialect uses this sound for the *ui* words.

The writers of the last two centuries have adopted a kind of haphazard compromise between old Scots and newer English spelling, but as their Scots speech gets thinner, more bookish and detached from real knowledge of historical Scots, the problems of writing it multiply.

A word may be said about the dialects of Scots, that is, the variant forms of the national speech of the fifteenth and sixteenth centuries, which are still spoken in the various regions. There are four main groups of these dialects, for convenience described geographically as Southern, Mid, Northern and Insular Scots.

Southern covers the old counties of Roxburgh, Selkirk and the eastern half of Dumfriesshire and has some things in common with the Cumbrian speech of England. As with the other dialects, many of the characteristics are acoustic, as intonation patterns and quality of vowels, which cannot easily be reproduced in writing. But the open pronunciation of *e* as in *bed, fell, leg, set, then*, etc., and of *i* in *bid, fill, pig, sit, thin*, and the slightly rounded back /ɑ/ as in *bag, hand*, *lang, mad,* are features; so are the pronunciations *away* (for the general Scots *awa*), *mey* /məi/, *hey, trey, sey,* for *me, he, tree, see/sea; twae, whae,* for *twa, wha; cow, now, how,* for *coo, noo, hoo* elsewhere; and the /ø/ sound still remains, as in *buit, mune, guid.*

At the other end of Scotland we have the Northern dialect, which begins just beyond Dundee and includes the area east of a line drawn from the mouth of the Tay to about Inverness, being at its most distinctive within the bounds of the new local government Grampian Region. Its main characteristic is the frequency of the *ee* /iː/ vowel which represents not only the *ui* in *guid* and *schule* (which become *gweed* and *skweel*), *bleed* for *bluid, seen* for *sune, peer* for *puir,* and so on, but also the common Scots *a* /e/ before *-ne,* as *een* for *ane, steen* for *stane, been* for *bane.* The back *a* is not rounded as in the other dialects, so that *hand* is *haan,* like German *Hahn,* and the *o* in words like *box* is more like English than the Mid Scots *boax.* Another feature is the use of *f* at the beginning of words for *wh,* as in *fat, far* (where), *fan* (when), *fa* (who), *fite* (white), *fussle* (whistle), *furl* (whirl), but note the exception *wheel.* The north-east has preserved many words which have dropped out of use elsewhere, as well as the frequent use of the diminutive, as in *mannie, wifie, housie, burnie, pannie, jougie* (little jug), etc. A subdivision of this speech persists in the north-eastern half of Caithness, which says *geed* and *skeel,* has a diphthong /ei/ in the *stane, bane* words, uses the diminutive in *-ag* (from Gaelic), as *bairnag, lassag,* and has also the Highland *r,* pronounced with the tip of the tongue slightly turned back, a feature, incidentally, which is spreading in the more fashionable parts of Edinburgh and Glasgow as an alternative to the ordinary trilled *r* of Scots and Scottish English.

The most important of the dialects is Mid Scots, spoken over the rest of Lowland Scotland from the Mull of Galloway to Dundee, important because three of the four cities and the chief industrial and populous areas are within its bounds; because most of our great writers, Henryson, Dunbar, Lyndsay, Douglas, Montgomerie, Knox, Ramsay, Fer-

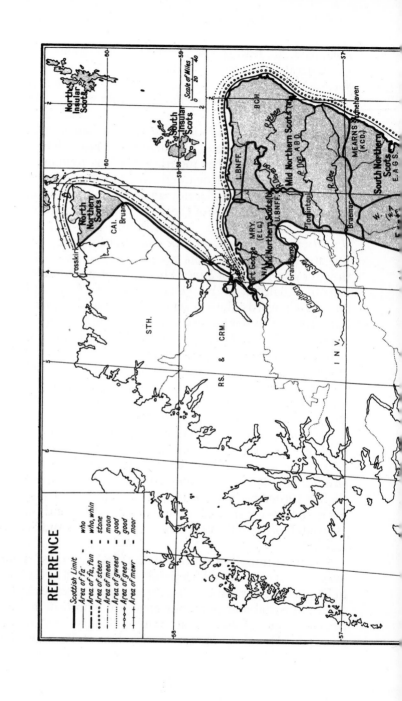

REFERENCE

———	Scottish Limit		
– – –	Area of fa	=	who
– ∙ – ∙ –	Area of fa, fun	=	who, whin
∘∘∘∘∘	Area of steen	=	stone
∙∙∙∙∙∙∙	Area of meen	=	moon
∙∙∙∙∙∙∙	Area of gweed	=	good
∘–∘–∘	Area of geed	=	good
+–+–+	Area of mewr	=	moor

North Insular Scots

South Insular Scots

Scale of Miles
0   20   40

North Northern Scots

CAI.
Crosskirk
Bruan

STH.

RS. & CRM.

BCH.

L.BNFF.

U.BNFF.

Mid Northern Scots (a)

MRY. (ELG.)
Fort George
Mid Northern Scots (b)

Grantown

R. Spey
R. Deveron

Mid Northern Scots (a)
ABD.

R. Don

Tomintoul

R. Dee

Braemar

MEARNS (KCD.)
Stonehaven

South Northern Scots
E.A.G.S.

I N V.

R. Findhorn

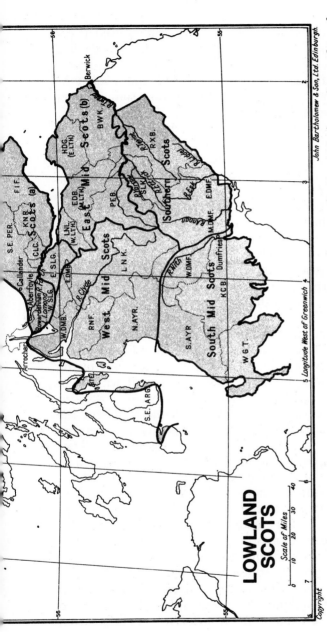

LOWLAND
SCOTS

Scale of Miles
0   10   20   30   40

Arrochar

S.E. ARG.

West Mid Scots

W.DMB.

Bowerdennan R.Fd.
Lomond
Aberfoyle
Callander

S.E. PER.
F.I.F.
KNR.
CLC. Scots (a)
E. SLG.
W. SLG.
E.DMB.

HDG.
(E.LTH)
Mid Scots (b)

BWK.

Berwick

LNL
(W.LTH)
East Mid Scots
EDB.
(MLTH)
PEB.

R.Clyde

R.Nith
SLK.
Southern Scots

RXB.

R. Ettrick
R. Teviot
R. Liddel

L.N.K.

RNF.

N.AYR.

S.AYR.

South Mid Scots

W.DMF.
Dumfries
M.DMF.
E.DMF.

K.C.B.

W.G.T.

R.B.N.T.

Copyright

3 | 4 Longitude West of Greenwich 5 | 6

John Bartholomew & Son, Ltd. Edinburgh.

The shaded portion covers the area in which Lowland Scots is spoken, and the boundaries within that region are those of the dialects. The dotted lines round the north-east coasts indicate the limits of the various criteria of the dialects, for which see the inset reference grid and pages 32-37.

gusson, Burns, Scott, Galt, Hogg, Stevenson, all used it; and because it is the direct descendant of the old metropolitan tongue of Scotland. The back *a* is usually well rounded, as in *haun* (hand), *caur* (car), *waurm* (warm), *auld* (old), *blaw*; the short *i* is everywhere lower than in English and sounds rather like the *u* in *but* or the *e* in *bet*.

Being spread over a wide area, this dialect has split into four subdivisions. The South Mid extends from the Solway Firth to the watershed into Clydesdale. The Clyde area itself, covering roughly the new Strathclyde Region, excluding Argyll except for enclaves in Kintyre, speaks West Mid Scots, familiar enough on radio and television from its Glasgow variety, which is evidently taken by the B.B.C. as their standard for Scots. There the constant diminutive is *wee*; the *ui* words now have the sound /ɪ/ or /e:/, as *din* (done), and *pair* (poor), in place of the /y/ sound which was then transferred to words pronounced /u:/ in English, as *you, true, blue*. This is less marked in the eastern division of this central dialect, East Mid Scots, which is itself subdivided into two, one south of the Forth in Lothian, Peeblesshire and Berwickshire, and the other north of the Forth in Fife, lowland Perthshire and west Angus. This last is characterised by the /ø/ for *ui*, the /e/, not /i/, in most words spelt with *ea* in English, and by having the largest number of vowels in Scots, a distinction it shares with Shetland. There the dialect, with that of Orkney, forms Insular Scots (sometimes called Norn, from *norroen*, Norwegian), essentially a Scots dialect superimposed on a Norwegian one which was spoken there until the seventeenth century and which has left a large substratum of Norse vocabulary—Shetland words like *bland* (whey drink), *kishie* (basket), *dim* (twilight), *haaf* (deep sea), *sillock* (coalfish), *moorit* (reddish brown), *noost* (boat-dock), *roo* (pluck a fleece), *voar* (spring season); Orkney words like *ayre* (beach), *arvo* (chickenweed), *bizzie* (cow-stall), *gamfer* (weather sign), *kreest* (squeeze), *kruggle* (crouch), *skaav* (scrape), *skurt* (lap), *tilter* (totter), *trowie* (sickly); and in both, the universal diminutive *peerie* (small). Similarities to Angus and Fife are due to the fact that it was chiefly from

36

these counties that the Scots settlers came when the islands came under Scottish suzerainty in the fifteenth century.

Much can be learned from the *Linguistic Atlas of Scotland*, now being issued from the University of Edinburgh, about the differences in sound and vocabulary between the dialects, which can identify their speakers. If you hear someone speak of boys and girls as *loons* and *quines*, you can tell from the map at once that he comes from Aberdeen-awa; otherwise he would have said *laddies* and *lassies*; for children generally, he will say *bairns* as most folk do up and down the east coast, whereas in the west they say *weans*, shortened from *wee anes*. Again, for the little finger the map gives *winkie* for Shetland and Orkney, *crannie* for the north-east, *curnie* for Fife, *creenack* for Inverness; in the west it is *wee finger*, but all over Scotland there is the word *pinkie* as well. A snowflake is *flag* in the north-east, *pile* in the West Mid area; soapy water is *graith* in the East Mid, *sapples* in the west; the grating over a street drain is *brander* in the north-east, *siver* in Mid Scots, and, especially in the East Mid region, *cundie*; the drain itself in the Glasgow area is the *stank*; broken china used by little girls as playthings is *lames* in the north-east, *piggies* in East Mid Scots and *wallies* in the west; mud and the muddy puddles on a road give the north-east *dubs*, farther south *gutters* or *glaur*. The earwig has a remarkable number of names: *forkietail* in the north, *clipshear* in Fife and Lothian, *gollach(er)* in Perth, Angus, Stirling and the west, possibly a borrowing from Gaelic, *scotchible* in the Berwick and Tweed areas. Examples could be extended almost indefinitely. There is certainly no lack of variety in Scots speech.

How Do You Say It in Scots?

To write a full grammar of a language now sorely in decay and so confused with standard English is beyond the scope of this chapter, but some of the main features of Scots are worth pointing out and some of the idioms peculiar to Scots, Scotticisms in fact, are listed for their interest and no doubt to the surprise of many Scots who may have used them all their lives, after the fashion of M. Jourdain, without realising the heinousness of their offence. One can only hope that those who feel mortified by the exposure are a diminishing few in a greater state of decay than the language itself.

There will have to be some old-fashioned grammar about this, and as schools have now abandoned this subject as being unpalatable and therefore unteachable, readers brought up under the new régime are advised simply to look at the examples used to explain the rules.

Nouns are much the same as in English with plurals in *-(e)s*, but some old plurals survive in Scots, as *een*, eyes, *shune*, shoes, *kye*, cows; and *thing* as a plural in *aathing*, everything, and *aa ither thing*, everything else.

In adjectives, a typical formation is by the addition of *like* or *kind* to almost any simple adjective (whereas English would use *-ish* or prefix it with *rather*), so *blacklike, doucelike*; *hetkind, sairkind,* the last two being used only predicatively after the verb *to be*. This *-kind* appears also in the words *siccan* (sic-kind), such, how; and *whaten* (what-kind), what, e.g. siccan a day as I've had; siccan cauld as it is!; whaten (a) big house is that? *Wiselike* often has the sense of respectable, sedate, decorous. Numerical adjectives end in *-t*, as *fift, saxt, nint,* though now only in the speech of old people.

The pronouns are as in English, but *thou*, often reduced to *tou,* was current in some parts of Scotland, especially in the Borders, till the First World War period, used as in Continental languages to close friends, children and young folk,

38

or to social inferiors, and still the regular usage in Shetland in the form *du*, and to a lesser extent in Orkney and the Black Isle. *Ye*, on the other hand, is universal, as well as *you*, with which it interchanges indiscriminately, though *ye* was originally the subject and *you* the object of a verb. *Scho* /ʃø/ is now obsolete and has been replaced by the English form *she*. It is not uncommon to hear the old form *hit* for *it* when spoken emphatically, and it survives also as the *hit* in games, of the one who does the seeking or catching. The indefinite pronoun 'one' is in Scots idiomatically *a body*: 'gin a body meet a body'. Everybody is *aabody*.

The reflexive pronoun is *himsel, hersel, themsel* or *-sels* or sometimes *theirsel*, which can for emphasis be altered to *the sel o him*, etc., and *lane* can also be substituted for *sel*, as *him lane, their lane(s)*; 'she sat there aa her lane'.

Modern Scots also preserves three demonstrative pronouns with peculiar Scots forms, while English has reduced them to two. The plural of *this* is *thir* in most Mid dialects of Scots but *this* in the north-east; the plural of *that* is *thae*, but again *that* in the north-east. The third form, especially common in the west, and usually indicating something a little more remote from the speaker than *that*, is *yon*, or in some eastern dialects, the mixed form *thon*. Another pronoun is *ilk*, the same word in its Scots and northern English form as *each*, now more commonly in the form *ilka* (for *ilk a(ne)*), as 'Ilka lassie has her laddie'. There is, by the by, another *ilk* = 'same', used in titles where a landowner's surname is the same as that of his estate: so 'Swinton of that ilk', meaning 'Swinton of Swinton'. This usage was later misinterpreted, and *ilk* has come to be used as a noun = 'sort, type'.

The relative pronoun in modern Scots has been simplified to *that* or *at* (Norse *at*), the form *whilk*, corresponding to English *which*, being now obsolete. *Wha* (who), *wham* (whom) are not so used in idiomatic Scots, so that *the man wha* is a literary adaptation of English, as in 'Scots wha hae, Scots wham Bruce . . .'. 'Whose' is expressed by *that his, that her*, as 'the man that I used tae work wi his son', 'the woman that her bairn's no weel', 'the house that ye can see the lums

39

o'(t)'. Sometimes the relative is omitted as in Burns's 'To a Haggis': 'Olio that wad staw a sow, or fricassee wad mak her spew'; 'I gae it tae the man was here yestreen'.

The reciprocating pronouns *one* and *other* have in Scots the forms *tane* and *tither* (due to wrong syllabling of *that ane* and *that ither*), as in 'The Twa Corbies': 'The tane unto the tither did say'; and where English says 'one another', Scots omits the 'one' as in 'they focht ither'; hence *throuither*, as an adjective = 'untidy, jumbled up'.

In Scots there is a tendency to keep the ending -*s*, which originates in a use of the possessive case in nouns, to form adverbs and which has almost disappeared in English except in *once, since, whence*. So in Scots we have *whiles*, sometimes, *ablins*, perhaps, *mebbies, geylies* (pretty much), *brawlies*, as well as *mebbe, geylie, brawlie*; and -*lins*, corresponding to English -*long*, in *endlins, sidelins*, also *halflins, newlins*. Scots will also use -*gate* or sometimes -*wey* for English *where* in *aagate, naewey, somegate, ilkawey. Whatwey* means 'why' or 'how', *what for*, 'why, for what reason' when used in questions. *And aa* means 'too, as well'.

As in most languages there are many emphatic words for 'very'; the commonest one is *gey* (French *gai*); *unco* (from *uncouth*), as in *the unco guid*, the rigidly righteous, and *brawlie* are now rather old-fashioned; *fair, richt*, are also common; *awfu* is more usual on the east side of Scotland; *fell* is characteristic of the Tayside Region; *byous*, excessively, is nearly obsolete. In 'at all' the *at* has been replaced by *of*, giving *ava*, like French *du tout*.

South of the Tay, the negative is *no*, short for the old Scots *nocht*, nought, not. North of the Tay it is *nae*, from original *nā*, but the *n't* of English, as in *don't, can't*, etc., is -*na, canna, maunna, dinna, winna, daurna, haena*. 'Too, excessively' is everywhere *ower*.

A very common adverb is *ben*, 'inwards, in or into the centre or more private part of a house, farther in'. This was originally *beinnan*, 'inwards', as opposed to *beūtan*, 'outwards', and dates from the time when cottages, like Burns's birthplace, had only two rooms, one opening from the outside, the *but*, and the other, the *ben*, opening off the *but*. Hence the expression *a but-and-ben*. *To be far ben wi* is used metaphorically for 'to be well in with, be in the good graces of'.

Prepositions, on the other hand, the wee words that you must not end a sentence with, can be very troublesome and not easy to systematise, as so much of their usage is idiomatic with particular words and phrases. Words beginning in English with *be-* have frequently *a-* (from *on*) in Scots, as *afore, ahint, aneath, aside, ayont, atween,* and Scots has a fondness for compound prepositions and adverbs as *inower* and *outower, inby* and *outby, aff o, on til, in o* and *out o,* of place as well as motion, so that *intae* or *intil* can be used alike for *in* and *into,* as in 'What's intil't?' Hence we say *inower the bed,* 'in bed', *outower the door,* 'out of doors', *it's in o the box, he fell aff o the ledder, he cam inby the house,* 'he dropped in to see us'. Another element in compounding is *-hand* as in *nearhand,* near, *efterhand,* after, so that 'after all' in Scots sounds rather like *efter and aa.* Another preposition often heard is *fornent,* meaning 'opposite to, facing', as 'His shop's fornent the garage'. This is also a compound, of *for(e)* and *anent,* which is used by itself in some dialects (the first four letters being a reduced version of *on even* with the unetymological *-t* that appears in *against* or *amidst*), and which has survived in the language of Scots law in the sense of 'concerning, in reference to'. *With* is regularly *wi,* but *without* is *athout* or, idiomatically, *wantin,* from the verb *want,* 'to lack': 'He cam hame wantin his breeks.'

One cause of confusion with the prepositions is that in Scots *of* and *on* are both generally contracted to *o* with a consequent mixture of their usages, so that *aff o* is for *off of,* *on o* for *on on, out o* for *out of,* but often re-expanded to *outen.*

But many of the difficulties are idiomatic, English using one preposition and Scots another; so we say *marriet on* (to), *angry at* (with), *ower* (out of) *the window, in* (as) *a present, wait on* (for), *cry on* (call to) *sit into* (nearer) *the fire, feart for* (afraid of), and of course with verbs, where the equivalent Scots may have a different construction, as *mind o,* remember, *lippen til,*

41

trust, depend on, *spier at,* ask.

Conjunctions—if readers under the age of fifty have heard of such things—are simpler. *If* was confused in Scots with the verb *gif,* give, in the sense of concede, and produced the now obsolete form *gif* and the modern *gin,* as in 'Gin a body'; *nor* is often used for *than, sin* for *since, or* for *ere,* before, till: 'He's aulder nor me; wait or I come.'

A much more complicated business is that of the indefinite article *a, an,* and the definite article *the.* In early Scots the usage with the first was precisely as in modern English, *a* before consonants, *an* before vowels, *a man, an apple,* except that *an* was usually written *ane.* This spelling became stylised for both *a* and *an* about the 1550s and lasted until the beginning of the eighteenth century; but this applied to spelling only, not pronunciation, so that what we see printed in Middle Scots texts as *ane,* as in the opening of Henryson's *Testament of Cresseid,* 'Ane doolie sessoun to ane cairfull dyte', should be read simply as *a,* despite what so many 'Scots' actors say. But when it means 'one', and is used with nouns, as a numerical adjective, it is now written *ae* and pronounced, according to dialect, /e:/ or /je:/, as 'There was ae winsome wench and walie', 'There was but ae bawbee left'. When it stands by itself as a pronoun, it is *ane* /en/ or /jen/: 'There was just ane broken'; 'Ane o them said tae me.' One hears occasionally, and reads oftener among our modern poets, 'There was yin man', but, like so much of today's speech in Scotland, that is neither good Scots nor good English.

The simple word *the* has its own peculiar role in Scots, for instance where English would use the appropriate possessive pronoun—*the wife, the brither, the fit, hand, to keep* or *lose the heid*—or even more frequently omit any qualifying word, as *awa tae the kirk, at the schuil, sittin at the table, sent tae the jile, up the stair, doun the toun, aff tae the* or *my bed, fish for the tea, the price o the milk and the butter's aye gaun up;* with names of diseases, *the measles, the jaundice;* of various activities and accomplishments, branches of learning, games, etc., as *she's takin lessons at the singin; he tuik up the fermin; guid at the*

French and the Science; a game at the fitba, the bouls (marbles), *the dams* (draughts), *the cairts.* It is common with *baith, maist, the baith* or *the maist o you,* or when English would have *a* as *in a shillin the piece, for the maitter o a pound or twa.*

There are also several historical usages which have survived sporadically as in some place-names to which *the* is prefixed locally, especially in the south-west of Scotland, as *the Troon, the Rhu, the Langholm*; or again with the numerals for any given year, those for the century often being omitted, *the sixteen hunder and forty-twa, the echty-nine,* now almost obsolete except in those memorable years of the Jacobite risings in the eighteenth century, *the Fifteen* and *the Forty-five.* On the other hand, English uses *the* and Scots omitted it regularly before the names of rivers, as Burns in 'Irwin, Lugar, Aire and Doon, Naebody sings', and as the Anglo-Saxons did. But this is restricted today to place-names as *Bridge of Allan, Bridge of Dee.* Again, Scots has replaced the English prefix *to-* with *the* in *thegither, the day, the morn* (tomorrow), and on the analogy of the last two in some northern dialects, *the streen* (for *yestreen, yestereven*), yesterday; or English *this* in *the year.*

Finally, in the verb there are again distinctions between Scots and English, originating fairly far back in the divergences of northern and southern Anglo-Saxon. In the earlier records the endings of the present tense indicative mood singular were, in the north: 1st person *-(e)*, 2nd person *-(i)s*, 3rd person *-(i)s*; and in the south, 1st person *-e*, 2nd *-est*, 3rd *-eth*; in the plural in the north *-(e)* for all persons, and in the south *-en.* It will be noticed that modern English has taken over *-(i)s* in the 3rd person singular from the north, and dropped the *-n* in the plural. Now we are left with Scots and English the same except for the 2nd person singular, which Burns again correctly renders in 'The Daisy': 'Thou lifts thy unassuming head' (not *lift'st*); 'Thou's met me in an evil hour' (not *hast*); and of course in Shetland *du kens,* etc.

But in the north this arrangement originally applied strictly to cases where the subject of the verb was a personal pronoun, *I, he, you,* etc., coming immediately in front of the verb itself. Where the subject was *not* a personal pronoun or the pronoun was separated by intervening words from the verb, the rule was that all persons ended in *-s* in the singular and plural alike. So when the Ettrick Shepherd sings how nice it is to meet a bonnie lassie 'when the kye comes hame', his Scots is as unexceptionable as his sentiments, because *kye* is not a pronoun; and so too is 'you that kens Latin', since *that* comes between *you* and *kens*, in contradistinction to 'Gin ye ken Latin'; or again: 'It's them that has tae dae the orra jobs.'

In older Scots the present participle, which is an adjective, ended in *-and*, often reduced to *-an*, while the gerund, which describes the action of the verb and is a noun, ended in *-in(g)*. Burns, as we have seen, noted the fact. In some dialects in the far south and the far north a quick ear may still notice some difference in the vowel of the second syllable of *singin* in: 'She gaed singin /-ən/ doun the road' and 'She's takin lessons in singin /-in/', but in the rest of Scotland the distinction is now quite blurred in speech and was ignored altogether in writing till the Lallans poets tried to revive it.

Scots, like English, has two main types of verbs, strong and weak. Strong verbs are those which alter their vowels in the past tense and past participles, like *bear, bore, borne; sit, sat; bind, bound; ring, rang, rung*. Past participles end in *-(e)n*, though this has sometimes dropped off, especially in English, as in *got* compared with Scots and American *gotten*, Scots more frequently preserving it, as in *sitten, putten, bidden, hauden* (held), *strucken, fochten* (fought). In weak verbs vowel change is exceptional, but the constant characteristic is the past tense and past participle ending in *-(e)d*, or *-t*, in Scots *-(i)t* or *-d*, as *grip, grippit; walk, walkit; hear, heard*, Scots *hard; keep, keepit; tell, tellt, telld*, or *tauld*.

In Old Scots *literary* usage an alternative way of indicating the past tense was by using the word *gan* (the past tense of *gin*, to begin), so that *he gan gae* was equivalent to *he went*. This *gan* was later confused with *can* and *can gae* became very common in Middle Scots poetry; then to emphasise the pastness of the action and no doubt to avoid confusion with *can*, to be able, its past tense was used; and so *couth* (could) *gae* and *can gae* had both the same meaning of *went*. This usage has been obsolete since the seventeenth century, but one relic survives in the late past tense form *begoud*, still used in some dialects for *began*, via the *can/couth* usage: 'She begoud tae greet.'

The Anglo-Saxon strong verb has been divided by the grammarians into seven classes and the weak verbs into three, but in the transition into Middle English these became confused—strong verbs might become weak and weak strong—and there is hardly a verb in modern English which still belongs entirely to its original class. Besides, Scots and English have gone their separate ways in this, as the following examples of the Scots conjugation of verbs will show. It will be noticed that some verbs have both strong and weak forms, especially in the past participle.

bide (stay)	bade	bidden
bind	band	bun(d)
burn	brunt	brunt
burst	brast, burstit	burst(en)
cast	cuist	cuisten, casten
catch	catcht	catcht
chuse	chase(t)	chosen
choice	choist	choist
clim(b)	clam, climt	climt
creep	creepit	creepit
	crap	cruppen
come	cam	come
	comed	comed
drive	drave	driven
eat	ate	aten
fecht	focht	fochten
fesh (fetch)	fuish	feshen, fuishen
find	fand	fund
gae	gaed	gane
	went	went

45

gie	gae, gied	gien, gied
greet (weep)	grat	grutten
haud	held	hauden
hae	had	had, haen
hurt	hurtit	hurtit
lat (let)	luit	latten, luitten
lauch	laucht	laucht
	leuch	lauchen
lowp	lowpit	lowpit
	lap	luppen
pit (put)	pat	putten
quit	quat	quitten
saw (sow)	sawed, shue	sawn
shue (sew)	shued	shued, shuen
slide	slade	slidden
sleep	sleepit	sleepit
steal	stole, staw	stown
	stealt	stealt
stand	stuid	stuid(en)
	stant	stant
stick	stack	stucken
	stickit	stickit
strick	strack	strucken
strive	strave	striven
soum (swim)	soumed	soumed
soup (sweep)	soupit	soupit
tak	tuik	tane
teach	teacht	teacht
thrash	thruish	thrashen, thruishen
wash	wuish	washen, wuishen
wind	wan(d)	wun(d), wundit
work	wrocht	wrocht

Pruive has also the strong past participle *pruiven* which survives in the third alternative verdict open to a Scottish jury in doubt about a conviction—*not proven*/prøvn/.

The auxiliary verbs *shall, will, may, can, maun* (must), *hae*, are used much as in English. *Sal*, the historical Scots form, is

46

nearly obsolete, but is occasionally heard in the negative *sanna*, and reduced to *se* in the expressions *Ise warrant, Ise uphaud*, for 'I'll bet'. It is a truism to say that Scots speakers get *shall* and *will* mixed up, and with some reason, if one takes the usage of the eighteenth- and nineteenth-century English as the standard, but in fact in colloquial English today, under the influence of dialects and American English, *will* is rapidly encroaching on *shall*, and approximating to the looser usage of Scots. In the first person *will* is used of simple futurity and *shall*, if used at all, of determination, as 'I will see you the morn', 'I shall pit a stop tae that, whatever happens'. In the second and third persons *will* can indicate the speaker's determination: 'Ye will dae what I bid you', 'Na, I winna (or sanna)', 'Ay but ye will'.

A common usage, frequently associated with Highland speakers, is the use of *will be* or *will have been* in tentative statements or questions, as 'You will be from Edinburgh? Will you have been living there long?'

In the west and south of Scotland *can* is treated as a verb on its own and may be governed by other auxiliaries, as 'Will ye can dae it for me? Na, I'll no can'. There is also an idiom with the verb *get*, when followed by the past participle: 'I couldna get sleepit for the midges', 'We couldna get sitten doun = we couldn't find seats'.

Finally, a rather odd use of the original past participle of *aw* (owe) to mean 'own' occurs in the expression *Wha's aucht?* 'Who owns, to whom does . . . belong?' with the answer *N's aucht it*.

What Is Left of It?

The vocabulary of Scots is much more extensive than might be supposed, if we include all words recorded over the last six centuries, now obsolete or not. *The Dictionary of the Older Scottish Tongue* and *The Scottish National Dictionary* between them must deal with well over 50,000 words peculiar to Scots either in form or meaning. Where did they come from?

As a dialect of Anglo-Saxon naturally by far the greater part of the vocabulary of Scots derives from there and is shared with English, though the pronunciation may differ sometimes as in the italicised words, like man, wife, son, *daughter*, cat, dog, horse, fire, *house, wood, food*, drink, bread, come, *go*, say, think, *do*, in, *out*, up, *down, red*, white, green, *good*, bad, thick, thin, sit, *climb, run*, and so on. Some words have survived in Scots which have disappeared in standard English, as *bield*, shelter, *blate*, shy, *cleuch*, ravine, *dwine*, decay, *gloaming*, twilight, *greet*, weep, *hauch*, river meadow, *heuch*, cliff, *lout*, stoop, *smeddum*, fine meal, pith, energy, *swick*, swindle, *wersh*, insipid—for all of which see the dictionaries.

Gaelic came into direct contact with Anglo-Saxon in the 900s, and throughout this century, and ever since, Gaelic words have trickled into the vocabulary of Scots, though in surprisingly small number. The earliest were chiefly of geographical terms: *bog, cairn*, heap of stones, rocky hill, *craig*, cliff, *loch, glen, strath*, and the word *airt*, a point of the compass, as in Burns's 'O' a' the airts the wind can blaw'. Another early Gaelic word is *kain*, rent paid in kind, which survived until about a hundred years ago in reference to poultry paid to the laird; *fail*, a sod, which goes back through Gaelic to the Latin word *vallum*, a rampart (of turf), and was undoubtedly taken into Gaelic from the Roman wall across Central Scotland. *Caber*, a beam, rafter, recorded in Scots about 1500, is still used in the phrase *tossing the caber*. Other borrowings are *capercailie*, the wood grouse, literally 'woodhorse', *caper* representing the old Celtic word that appears in French as *cheval*; *partan*, the edible crab; *sonsie*, lucky, happy, jolly, and now specifically plump; *clan*, Gaelic for a family; *clarsach*, a harp, now again a fashionable musical instrument in the Lowlands; *crine*, to shrink, shrivel; *cranreuch*, hoarfrost, as in Burns's 'To a Mouse'; *cateran*, robber; *ingle*, apparently originally a taboo word for fire, now meaning the fireside; *ptarmigan*, an extraordinary Greek-style spelling for Gaelic *tarmachan*, the mountain grouse; *tocher*, dowry; and *slogan*, originally a war cry.

The opening up of the Highlands during the Jacobite period of the eighteenth century brought more Gaelic words, mainly referring to Highland objects, into Scots and not infrequently into English as well, like *claymore*, the broadsword, *filibeg*, the kilt, *pibroch*, *sporran*, purse, *usquebae*, aquavitae, almost literally watered down to *whisky*, and *gillie*, a sportsman's attendant, originally a lad, and surviving more phonetically in the form of *keelie*, a young townee, especially in Glasgow, implying a bit of a rough, a corner-boy, many of whom last century were young Highlanders uprooted by the Clearances. A more recent borrowing is *ceilidh*, a party with impromptu entertainment, a sing-song.

A more important source of Scots vocabulary arises from Old Norse, the language of the Vikings. The intake of Norse vocabulary into Northern English continued from 900 to 1150 and spilt over into Scotland as the Norman Conquest brought fresh settlers from England in the twelfth and thirteenth centuries. Norse had close affinities with, as well as differences from, Anglo-Saxon, instances of the latter being that in certain positions in a word Norse had *k* where Anglo-Saxon had the sound *ch* /tʃ/; hence correspondences like English *church, chest, churn, churl, birch, breeches, which, such, each, ditch, stitch, bench,* from Anglo-Saxon, and Scots *kirk, kist, kirn, carl* (man), *birk, breeks, whilk, sic, ilk, dyke, steek, bink* from Norse. Somewhat similarly English has *sh* from Anglo-Saxon in *shrill, shriek, mash,* or *dge* in *bridge, ridge, sedge*, compared with Scots *skirl, skriech, mask* (to make tea), *brig, rig, seg*, with Norse ancestors. Another distinction is that Scots has the sound *ow* /ʌ u/ where English has *ea* /i:/, as in *lowp* (Norse *hlaupa*) for *leap* (Anglo-Saxon *hlēapan*) and *cowp* (Norse *kaupa*, which gives the first element in the name *Copenhagen*), meaning to bargain or trade, corresponding to English *cheap* (and *Chipping* in place-names). English *own* had its Scots equivalent *awn* from Anglo-Saxon *āȝen*, but this Scots form has now been replaced by *ain*, from Norse *eiginn*.

The contribution of Norse to Scots (and Northern English dialects) in new words has been very considerable. Here are some: *at*, the relative pronoun = who, which; *big*, build; *blae*, blue, as in *blaeberry*; *brae*, the *brow* of a hill; *busk*, to dress, adorn; *carline*, an old woman, feminine form of *carl* above; *ettle*, to aim, intend; *eident*, industrious; *ferlie*, a wonder, strange sight; *drucken*, drunken (not a corruption of the English but from the Norse *drukinn*); *fike*, to fidget; *frae*, from; *gar*, to make, compel; *gate*, road, as in many Scottish street-names, *Gallowgate, Canongate, Trongate, Overgate*; *gimmer*, a female lamb; *gowk*, a fool, from Old Norse *gauk*, cuckoo; *graith*, tools, equipment, soap-suds; *hing*, from the Norse correspondence to English *hang*; *host*, cough; *low*, flame; *luif*, palm of the hand; *kilt*, from a Norse verb = to tuck up; *neive*, fist; *rowan*, mountain ash; *skerrie*, isolated sea rock; *lug*, the ear; *rug*, to tug; *strae*, from Old Norse *strá* = Anglo-Saxon *strēaw*, English *straw*; *scug*, to hide, skulk; *til*, a very characteristic Scandinavian word for *to*; *stowp*, a drinking-vessel, probably best known from 'Auld Lang Syne'; *tike*, dog; *tyne*, to lose. Most of these words are in use to this day, attesting the importance of the Norse element.

All this of course is independent of the other Norse linguistic contact with Scotland in the north, Shetland, Orkney, and to a lesser extent Caithness, already mentioned.

The third source of borrowing, the biggest and most important of all, is from French, which came to Scotland in three distinct periods. The first was Norman French, the

50

French adopted by the Viking invaders of Northern France and brought to England by William the Conqueror in 1066. Thence, as we have seen, it percolated through Scotland in the course of the next hundred years.

Later on in England this type of French became very old-fashioned and ultimately died out, while the French of Paris and the central area of France supplanted it, not only as being more *à la mode* but as being nearer the speech of those parts of France which had come into the possession of the Angevin kings of England; this also spilt over into Scotland from the beginning of the fourteenth century. The differences between these varieties of French will sometimes explain the distinctions in form between Scottish and English borrowings. We have already noted how Norse speakers in England kept the sounds *k* and *g* and did not turn them into *ch* and *dge*; and that was true in France also. In consequence the Normans said *castel*, castle, *cacher*, catch, *roc*, *gardin*, *gartier*, where the Parisian says *château*, *chasser*, *roche*, *jardin*, *jarretière*. In most cases English has the earlier form, like *rock*, *cauldron*, *canon* (and of course sometimes both, as in *cattle* and *chattel*, *catch* and *chase*), while Scots has the Parisian forms *roche* (in poetry), *chalder*, a measure of grain contained in a cauldron, *chanoun*, obsolete except in the place-name Chanonry in the cathedral towns of Fortrose, Elgin and Aberdeen. But Scots has the earlier Norman form in *campioun*, often applied to Wallace, and also incidentally in *leal*, the older French form which later became *loyal*; cf. also *syver*, drain, with *sewer*, from two different French dialects.

Between them these two sources supply by far the greater part of the French vocabulary common to English and Scots. Some has now disappeared from standard English but survives in English dialects or Scots, like *ashet*, meat plate, *aumrie*, cupboard, *causey* (Parisian French *chausée*, altered in English to *causeway*), *cowp*, to capsize, *douce*, *grosert*, gooseberry, *houlet*, owl, *jigot*, leg of mutton, *lammer*, amber, *mavis*, thrush, *stank*, pool, drain, *tassie*, cup, *vieve*, life-like.

Again some words differ by following the different sound-laws of Scots and English, as *failyie*, fail, *fulyie*, foil, leaf, *spulyie*, spoil, *tulyie*, toil, *cunyie*, coin or quoin, *fenyie*, feign—most of these forms are now obsolete—*bouls*, marbles, *pouch*, pocket, *succar*, sugar, *drogs*, *creish*, grease, fat.

It is a common mistake to ascribe all this vocabulary to the third French source which also began to replenish Scots a century or so later—the Auld Alliance, first struck between Scotland and France in 1296. It was effective from about 1330 and lasted until the Reformation of 1560 when the new Protestant Scotland ruptured with Catholic France. To the earlier part of the period belong such borrowings as *affeir*, *effeir*, *feir*, appearance, bearing, especially in the old legal phrase *bodin in fere of weir*, in warlike array; *disjune*, breakfast; *purpie*, purple; *row*, street; *spairge*, splash, *vaig*, roam; *bonallie*, a send-off; *Bon-Accord*, the motto of Aberdeen. The sixteenth century gives *aippleringie*, southernwood; *dote*, endow; *fash*, bother; *sussy*, care, trouble (French *souci*); *visie*, to aim (*viser*); *vivers*, rations (*vivres*); *bajan* or *bejant*, as they say in the Universities of Aberdeen and St Andrews for English *freshman* (French *bec jaune*, 'yellow beak', or as we might say, using another Scots phrase, a 'green-horn'); *backet*, wooden container (*baquet*); *turner*, an old Scots twopenny piece (French *tournois*, from Tournai in Belgium); *howtowdie*, a fat chicken for the pot (French *hétoudeau*); *dams*, *dambrod*, the game and board for draughts (*jeu de dames*); *caddie*, a messenger, later a golfer's attendant (*cadet*); *gardyloo*, the warning call when slops were thrown out of the high Edinburgh houses at night, short for *prenez garde à l'eau*; and *hogmanay*, New Year's eve, from a Picardy dialect form of *aguillanneuf*, the children's begging-song on that night. And of course, unlike the first two lots, all the words in the last category are peculiar to Scots, as they bypassed England through the direct contacts of the Auld Alliance.

The establishment of the feudal system in Scotland involved the immigration of others besides the French. Already in England, in the wake of the Normans, Flemish wool-merchants and weavers, the most skilled of their kind in Western Europe, had set up their trades and crafts, and the Scottish kings gave them every encouragement to do the same in Scotland. Evidence for their settlement is in the surnames Fleming and Brebner (Brabanter) in the records for this period.

Early borrowings from Flemish Dutch in Scots are *cuit*, ankle; *craig* (the other *craig*), meaning neck; *crune*, to sing softly; *cran*, a crane, a tap; *bucht*, pen, enclosure; *coft*, bought, as in *Tam o' Shanter*; *dub*, pool, puddle; *geck*, a foolish or mocking gesture, to befool; *redd*, to clear up, tidy; *golf*, and many technical seafaring and military words, now obsolete.

In the fourteenth century a Scottish trading-post was established in the Netherlands which lasted until the end of the eighteenth century, and relationships were close for most of that period. Many more words came in in the late fifteenth and sixteenth centuries: *calland*, customer, merchant, chap, boy, common in the west of Scotland; *doit*, originally a small Dutch coin, something worthless; *dornick*, a kind of linen made in Doornik (Tournai) in Belgium; *dowp*, the backside; *kyte*, the belly; *loun*, a rascal, now the common Aberdeen word for a boy; *mutch*, a woman's cap; *mutchkin*, a pint measure; *pinkie*, the little finger; *skink*, shin (of beef); *scone*, for Dutch *schoonbrot*, fine bread. As the pioneers of the herring fishery in the eighteenth and nineteenth centuries, the Dutch used Shetland as a base and Shetland dialect has quite a number of Dutch words in addition.

Latin also makes its contribution to Scots independently of the huge number of words taken into English from Anglo-Saxon times onwards, directly and chiefly through the Church and also indirectly through French. We have seen some of this in the aureate diction of Dunbar and other poets. One Latin feature of Scots is the past participle in *-te*, which was not naturalised into *-ted* as it was in English weak verbs; so 'he was educate at the College', 'the meeting was constitute'; *execute*, *statute*, *depute*, and similarly *conjunct* for *conjoined*. Scots may also use one form of the root of the Latin (and French) verb where English will use another; so Scots *dispone* for English *dispose*, *expreme* for *express*, *promove* for *promote*. Scots law, which was developed from Roman law through Dutch in the seventeenth century, is especially full of Latin forms and terms, like *habite and repute*, originally past participles though now treated as nouns, *sopite, executor-dative, -nominate, sederunt, sist, nimious, interdict, homologate, obtemper*, to mention only a few. Some few words also have trickled in from school Latin, which after all was in daily use until the nineteenth century, words like *dominie*, for a schoolmaster, originally the Latin vocative = sir; *pandie*, a stroke with the tawse (leather strap), from the teacher's ominous command, *pande manum*, hold out your hand; *fugie*, a coward (from Latin *fugere*, to run away); and *dux*, the head boy or girl in a class.

Scots and English have a very great deal in common, yet in not a few cases Scots will use the same word in a different sense from English in what is generally called a Scotticism. In Scots a *crack* means a chat; *cripple* is as often used as an adjective as a noun, as in Cripple Dick; a *divider* is a serving-spoon or ladle; 'I doubt it'll be rain' implies in English 'I don't think rain is likely', whereas in Scots it means 'I'm afraid it is likely', like French *douter*, with the same force; in Scots you *find* a pain and *feel* a smell; *half four*, of time, means 3.30 as in Continental use, though by a confusion apparently originating in America it is now used incorrectly for 4.30; *flit*, like Scandinavian *flytta*, means to move house, and *flitting* is the removal; a *flower* is a bouquet—'The bride cairriet a flour'; *get* has several peculiarly Scots meanings: to find, as 'yes, I got it; I maun hae luitten it faa in the dark'; to be called, 'he aye gets Jockie'; to be allowed to go, 'can I get to the pictures?'; *haud* (hold) very frequently does duty for *keep*, as in 'hoo are ye haudin?', 'to haud gaun', 'to haud ower (move up)', 'a dram to haud you warm', 'to haud south (seek one's fortune in England)', 'haud a wee (wait a minute)'; *hurl*, a/to ride in a wheeled vehicle; *house* is applied in Scotland to any single family dwelling, as a *flat* itself (originally a Scotticism) in a block, whereas in England it usually denotes the whole building from foundation to roof; *mind* is to remember, a *minding* a memento; *next* in dates is idiomatically next but one (English *next,* the one immediately to come, being rendered as *this (Friday), (Friday) first); pig* is an earthenware vessel of any kind, originally from its shape, a usage which must have horrified the English visitor when told by the Scots chambermaid that she had 'putten a het pig in the bed'; *policies* are the grounds or parklands of an estate; *press,* a cupboard; *roof* is often used for *ceiling; seek* is to want, ask for: 'What's he seekin here? He socht the lend o a haimmer'; *shift anesel* is to change one's clothes; *a sair heid* is a headache, not the English *sore head,* a head covered with sores; *sort,* to repair; *spice,* pepper; *sober* means frail, in poor health, 'no weel' (Scots avoid saying 'ill'): 'He's been sober for weeks'; *stop,* to reside: 'They stop near the herbour'; *travel,* to go on foot; *weave,* to knit, especially in North Scotland, for which in Shetland they say *mak; want* is to lack, be in need of: 'The teapot wantit the lid', 'That laddie wants a skelpin'; *word* is the sound of one's voice: 'I kent him by his word.' And there are many more, but no doubt these are enough to be going on with for those who want to brush up their Scots.

Readers may have noticed that not a few of the words already mentioned, like *clan, whisky, crune, scone, golf, caddie, flat, raid,* have been adopted from Scots into English, and especially in the eighteenth and nineteenth centuries quite a number more were borrowed from the North, as *glamour, wraith, gruesome, stalwart,* from Scott, *feckless, flunkey, outcome, shortcoming,* from Carlyle. Other borrowings include golfing terms, like *tee, stymie, foursome,* the medical term *croup,* the Scots law terms, originally from French, *relevant* and *irrelevant;* geology, very much a Scottish science, pioneered by Hutton and Lyell, gave *kaim* and *drumlin; tweed,* by a happy mistake for *tweeled,* has extended its range beyond the Anglo-Saxon speaking world; and among other everyday English words of Scottish origin are *fogie, heckle, cosy, gloaming, rampage, eerie, canny* and *uncanny, pet, blackmail* (though the practice is not claimed as a Scottish invention), *dinky, shortbread, pony, spate;* and it was a Scotsman who coined the name of the typical Englishman, John Bull!

What Is Its Future?

Modern Scots rarely matches up to the description and criteria we have been prescribing above. Like dialects everywhere, it is under the severest pressure from the standard language and is rapidly losing its historic forms and structure through constant confusion with the official speech. Scots and English forms are jumbled up haphazardly so that a clear and consistent pattern can no longer be traced, and a systematic grammar has gone out of the window. Modern Scottish writers, striving for realism, reproduce this speech faithfully, but one may question how far it is Scots at all and not merely a kind of broken English. This is especially true of the speech of the industrial areas, where the influence of Highland and Anglo-Irish dialect, the new vocabulary of industrialism imported from England, the general currency of standard and substandard and slang English, particularly on the social strata of the towns, have all combined to attenuate and even obliterate Scots.

The two following extracts will illustrate what is meant, the first from Gordon Williams's *From Scenes Like These*, ix (1968):

> "So ah says tae him, listen here, mister, ah says, if ye think ye kin talk tae me like that ye've got anuther think comin', so ye huv. I wis fair livid, so I wis, richt enough. A big strappin fella like him tellin me whut fur! I felt like cloutin him ower the heid wi ma message-bag."

Or this from William McIlvanney's *Remedy is None*, xiv (1966):

> 'He was standin' facin' his own goal too. He trapped it and turned in the wan movement. An' then without stoppin' he brought it right past the back, just as if he

wisny there. He moved in to about the corner o' the box, an' the centre-half cut right across. His right foot was still in line wi the centre-half an' he blutered it wi his left. Really low an' right inside the post. Inch perfect. The goalie was naewhere. No chance.'

The picture of Scots in the previous chapters, therefore, is more idealistic than realistic today. Few native Scots speakers would use all the forms or expressions recorded above; the younger they are or the nearer they live to a city or industrialised area, the less idiomatic their Scots is likely to be. It has been calculated that about one-third of the vocabulary, for instance, has disappeared between one generation and the next, so that by the end of this century very little indeed will be left.

And that brings us to a consideration of the future of Scots and of the arguments started up by the Scottish Renaissance and Lallans movements in the 1920s. The chief exponent, C. M. Grieve, in the persona of 'Hugh MacDiarmid', argued that the basis of Scottish poetry during the last two centuries had been too narrow to compass the themes demanded by our age of transition, uncertainty and revolution; that the Scots poet cannot find his true medium of expression except in Scots; and that modern Scots speech is inadequate of itself to convey the message of modern poetry. It could expand its vocabulary partly by going back into its own past (in Grieve's case often via the Scottish dictionary) and reviving the language of the medieval poets, by inventing new forms and by borrowing from other tongues, even English, if need be. This had been a poetic policy as far back as Gavin Douglas in his translation of the *Aeneid*; Stevenson avowed it again in his introduction to *Underwoods* and Joyce had done it in a big way for English in *Ulysses* and *Finnegan's Wake*. There are, besides, plenty of analogies for this type of linguistic movement abroad, in Norway, The Faeroes, Yugoslavia, Israel, South Africa, and in some respects Switzerland also.

In pursuance of his dogma Grieve published his first work in this new vein, *Sangschaw* (1925), and no one now disputes its first-rank quality. Though it was looked on askance in Scotland, as one would expect, foreign critics treated it with understanding; and there can be no doubt that at one blow he had lifted Scots out of its rut and given it new intellectual and philosophical significance.

Grieve continued his linguistic experiments in *Penny Wheep*, culminating in *A Drunk Man Looks at the Thistle* (1926), his high-water mark in Scots.

From *Sangschaw*:

'Ae weet forenicht i the yow-trummle
I saw yon antrin thing,
A watergaw wi its chitterin licht
Ayont the on-ding;
An I thocht o the last wild look ye gied
Afore ye deed!

There was nae reek i the laverock's hoose
That nicht—an nane in mine;
But I hae thocht o that foolish licht
Ever sin syne;
An I think that mebbe at last I ken
What your look meant then.'

Forenicht, evening; *yow-trummle*, cold days in July causing trembling in sheep; *watergaw*, fragmentary rainbow; *antrin*, odd, occasional, here used = weird; *chitterin*, shivering; *ayont*, beyond; *on-ding*, downpour; *reek*, smoke; *laverock*, lark. The phrase, taken from Wilson's grammar of the dialect of Strathearn, means it was a wild, windy night.

From *A Drunk Man*:

'I tae ha'e heard Eternity drip water
(Aye water, water!), drap by drap
On the ae nerve, like lichtnin, I've become
And heard God passin' wi' a bobby's feet
Ootby in the lang coffin o' the street
—Seen stang by chitterin' knottit stang loup oot

58

Uncrushed by the echoes o' the thunderin' boot,
Till a' the dizzy lint-white lines o' torture made
A monstrous thistle in the space aboot me,
A symbol o' the puzzle o' man's soul
—And in my agony been pridefu' I could still
Tine nae least quiver or twist, watch ilka point
Like a white-het bodkin ripe my inmaist hert,
And aye wi' clearer pain that brocht nae anodyne,
But rose forever to a fer crescendo
Like eagles that ootsoar wi' skinklan' wings
The thieveless sun they blin'
    —And pridefu' still
That yont the sherp wings o' the eagles fleein'
Aboot the dowless pole o' Space,
Like leafs aboot a thistle-shank, my bluid
Could still thraw roses up
    —And up!'

Stang, throb, pang; *loup*, leap; *lint-white*, flaxen; *skinklan*, gleaming; *thieveless*, weak, powerless, thewless; *dowless*, feeble, probably confused with *doless*, devoid of activity; *shank*, stalk.

By 1936 the tide had receded and Edwin Muir in his *Scott and Scotland* stated the case against Scots and for English in literature with force and insight. He argued pessimistically the hopelessness of the case for continuing a distinct literature in a country where there is 'no organic community to round off the writer's conceptions, no major literary tradition to support him, nor even a faith among the Scots themselves that it was possible or desirable'. As regards the language problem proper he goes on to say that poetry arises when intellect and emotion fuse on equal terms and that this is not possible when the writer feels in *one* language and thinks in *another*. 'Scots poetry can only be revived when Scotsmen begin to think *naturally* in Scots. The curse of Scottish literature is the lack of a whole language, which finally means the lack of a whole mind.' And in answer to

Grieve's nationalism, Muir talks of the vain and agonising attempt to remake 'the broken image of a lost kingdom'.

During the war a new race of poets, among them William Soutar, Sydney Goodsir Smith, Robert Garioch, and Douglas Young, who popularised the term *Lallans* (Lowlands speech, as in Burns's 'Epistle to William Simson'), published their verses and reopened the controversy which still goes on.

One argument basic to the call for a revival of Scottish literature was that of T. S. Eliot to the effect that 'every literature needs refreshment from two sources, its own past and contemporary literature elsewhere', and in regard to the first in Scotland that involves a working knowledge of Scots.

A real weakness of the Lallans movement has been that the writers have restricted themselves almost entirely to *poetry*. In contrast to poetry, however, continuity in Scots prose was broken in the sixteenth century. There are no real models after that date and the medieval prose of a feudal society cannot be simply adapted to the needs of modern industrial life, having missed the evolution which English underwent in the intervening four centuries. Assuming the desirability of the attempt in the first place, to resuscitate Scots prose would require much experimental writing, beginning perhaps with the short story, and one may remember that one of the world's greatest short stories, Scott's 'Wandering Willie's Tale', was just such an experiment, which Stevenson followed in 'Thrawn Janet' and 'The Tale of Tod Lapraik'. Galt's efforts at a hybrid style point in the general direction of the solution, and he had some minor imitators in the nineteenth century. It was in the 1930s, however, that Lewis Grassic Gibbon in his *Scots Quair* tackled the problem anew in a manner not unlike Galt's, reproducing the rhythms and cadences and idioms of the North-East dialect but for the most part avoiding the local grammatical forms and most of the vocabulary, as in this passage from *Sunset Song*:

'Cuddiestoun and his wife sat opposite her, it was like watching a meikle collie and a futret at meat, him gulping down everything that came his way and a lot that didn't, he would rax for that; and his ugly face, poor stock, fair shone and glimmered with the exercise. But Mistress Munro snapped down at her plate with sharp quick teeth, her head never still a minute, just like a futret with a dog nearby. They were saying hardly anything, so busied they were, but Ellison next to them had plenty to say, he'd taken a dram over much already and was crying things across the table to Chris, Mistress Tavendale he called her at every turn; and he said that she and Mistress Ellison must get better acquaint. Maybe he'd regret that the morn, if he minded his promise; and that wasn't likely. Next to him was Kirsty and the boys and next to that the minister's table with Alec Mutch and his folk and young Gordon; a real minister's man was Alec, awful chief-like the two were, but Mistress Mutch sat lazy as ever, now and then she cast a bit look at Chris out of the lazy, gley eyes of her, maybe there was a funniness in the look that hadn't to do with the squint.

Up at Rob's table an argument rose, Chris hoped that it wasn't religion, she saw Mr Gordon's wee face pecked up to counter Rob. But Rob was just saying what a shame it was that folk should be shamed nowadays to speak Scotch—or they called it Scots if they did, the split-tongued sourocks! Every damned little narrow-douped rat that you met put on the English if he thought he'd impress you—as though Scotch wasn't good enough now, it had words in it that the thin bit scraichs of the English could never come at. And Rob said You can tell me, man, what's the English for sotter or greip, or smore, or pleiter, gloaming or glunching or well-kenspeckled? And if you said gloaming was sunset you'd fair be a liar; and you're hardly that, Mr Gordon.

But Gordon was real decent and reasonable. You can't help it, Rob. If folk are to get on in the world nowadays, away from the ploughshafts and out of the pleiter, they must use the English, orra though it be. . . .

61

There was nothing on the land but work, work, work, and chave, chave, chave, from the blink of day till the fall of night, no thanks from the soss and sotter, and hardly a living to be made.'

Cuddiestoun, a farm-name, extended in Scots idiom to indicate the farmer himself; *futret*, weasel, north-east form of *whitrat*, 'white rat'; *rax*, stretch; *stock*, chap, 'bloke'; *Mistress* indicates the common Scots pronunciation = English *Missus*; *acquaint*, past participle, from French *accoint*; *chieflike*, intimate, pally, cf. *Proverbs*, xvi, 28; *gley*, squint; *Scotch/Scots*, Gibbon has got the forms the wrong way round for his argument. *Scotch* is the English form of the Scottish *Scots* (see p. 5); *sourock*, sorrel, a sour person; *scraich*, shriek; *sotter*, a mess; *greip*, drain in a byre; *smore*, smother; *pleiter*, mire, dirty messy work; *glunch*, scowl; *well-kenspeckled*, Gibbon means *kenspeckle*, conspicuous; *chave*, north-east form of *taw*, to toil and moil, work laboriously.

He is thus not so much writing in Scots but rather strongly Scotticising his English, and this cautious approach is possibly the most prudent course at the moment, even if the dignity of the old curial Scots is not there. And it is really *that* that has to be restored to the language. One must intellectualise the prose as well as the poetry.

Meanwhile Scots will continue to be spoken *diminuendo* in familiar circles, especially in the outlying areas like the Borders, Ayrshire, Angus, the Moray Firth area and in Shetland; and the Scots voice will continue to utter the English language in its own peculiar way. But it cannot be restored until the Scots know what it is and want it so, and that means that it must be given an assured and permanent place in our schools and colleges. Certainly no other European nation would tolerate anything less.

Reading List

Chambers's Encyclopedia (Article on Scottish language by Sir William Craigie and A. J. Aitken) (1967 edition).

Chambers's Scots Dictionary (Ed. A. Warrack) (Introduction by W. Grant) (1911).

The Dialect of Robert Burns, Sir James Wilson (1926).

The Dialect of the Southern Counties of Scotland, J. A. H. Murray (Still the fundamental work, though outdated in details) (1876).

The Dialects of Central Scotland, Sir James Wilson (1923).

Dictionary of the Older Scottish Tongue, Sir William Craigie and A. J. Aitken (Now at the letter P. The definitive work for the period before 1700) (1929-   ).

Etymological Dictionary of the Scottish Language, J. Jamieson (The pioneer work, now out of date) (Editions from 1808 to 80).

The Linguistic Atlas of Scotland, Scots section, J. Y. Mather and H. H. Speitel (Vol. 1, 1975; Vol. 2, 1977).

Lowland Scotch, Sir James Wilson (1915).

Manual of Modern Scots, W. Grant and J. M. Dixon (A full analysis of the pronunciation and grammar of present-day Scots and its various dialects) (1920).

The Scottish National Dictionary, W. Grant and D. Murison (For the period from 1700 to date. Important introduction) (1929-76).

Specimens of Middle Scots, G. Gregory Smith (Important for spelling and syntax and as illustrating linguistic ideas in Middle Scots) (1902).